The Ramones

American Punk Rock Band

Library Ed. ISBN-13:
978-0-7660-3031-2
Paperback ISBN-13:
978-0-7660-3623-9

Library Ed. ISBN-13:
978-0-7660-3236-1
Paperback ISBN-13:
978-1-59845-210-5

Library Ed. ISBN-13:
978-0-7660-3379-5
Paperback ISBN-13:
978-1-59845-212-9

Library Ed. ISBN-13:
978-0-7660-3232-3
Paperback ISBN-13:
978-1-59845-211-2

Library Ed. ISBN-13:
978-0-7660-3234-7
Paperback ISBN-13:
978-1-59845-208-2

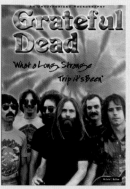

Library Ed. ISBN-13:
978-0-7660-3028-2
Paperback ISBN-13:
978-0-7660-3620-8

Library Ed. ISBN-13:
978-0-7660-3029-9
Paperback ISBN-13:
978-0-7660-3621-5

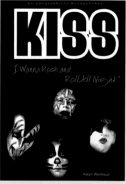

Library Ed. ISBN-13:
978-0-7660-3027-5
Paperback ISBN-13:
978-0-7660-3619-2

Library Ed. ISBN-13:
978-0-7660-3026-8
Paperback ISBN-13:
978-0-7660-3618-5

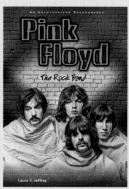

Library Ed. ISBN-13:
978-0-7660-3030-5
Paperback ISBN-13:
978-0-7660-3622-2

Library Ed. ISBN-13:
978-0-7660-3233-0
Paperback ISBN-13:
978-1-59845-213-6

Library Ed. ISBN-13:
978-0-7660-3231-6
Paperback ISBN-13:
978-1-59845-209-9

The Ramones

American Punk Rock Band

Brian J. Bowe

REBELS OF ROCK

Enslow Publishers, Inc.
40 Industrial Road
Box 398
Berkeley Heights, NJ 07922
USA

http://www.enslow.com

To Niel Carlson.

Library of Congress Cataloging-in-Publication Data

Bowe, Brian J.
    The Ramones : American Punk Rock Band / Brian J. Bowe.
        p. cm. — (Rebels of rock)
    Includes bibliographical references, discography, and index.
    Summary: "A biography of American punk rock band the Ramones"—Provided by publisher.
    ISBN-13: 978-0-7660-3233-0
    ISBN-10: 0-7660-3233-7
    1. Ramones (Musical group)—Juvenile literature. 2. Punk rock musicians—United States—
Biography—Juvenile literature. I. Title.
    ML3930.R26B68 2010
    782.42166092'2—dc22
    [B]   2008040362

ISBN-13: 978-1-59845-213-6 (paperback ed.)

Printed in the United States of America

052010 Lake Book Manufacturing, Inc., Melrose Park, IL

10 9 8 7 6 5 4 3 2 1

To Our Readers: This book has not been authorized by The Ramones or its successors.

We have done our best to make sure all Internet Addresses in this book were active and appropriate when we went to press. However, the author and the publisher have no control over and assume no liability for the material available on those Internet sites or on other Web sites they may link to. Any comments or suggestions can be sent by e-mail to comments@enslow.com or to the address on the back cover.

Every effort has been made to locate all copyright holders of material used in this book. If any errors or omissions have occurred, corrections will be made in future editions of this book.

♻ Enslow Publishers, Inc., is committed to printing our books on recycled paper. The paper in every book contains 10% to 30% post-consumer waste (PCW). The cover board on the outside of each book contains 100% PCW. Our goal is to do our part to help young people and the environment too!

Photo Credits: Associated Press, pp. 91, 97; Roberta Bayley/Redferns/Getty Images, p. 56; Ian Dickson/Redferns/Getty Images, p. 23; Kevin Estrada/Retna Ltd., USA, p. 76; Everett Collection, p. 58; GAB Archives/Redferns, p. 32; Dale Harris, p. 89; Hulton Archive/Getty Images, p. 20; Robert Knight, p. 83; Magnolia/Photofest, p. 11; Linda Matlow/Rex USA, courtesy Everett Collection, p. 70; Michael Ochs Archives/Getty Images, pp. 6, 37; © Paramount/courtesy Everett Collection, p. 79; Ed Perlstein/Redferns/Getty Images, p. 50; April Roberts, p. 95; Gus Stewart/Redferns, pp. 17, 26; Gai Terrell/Redferns, p. 63; WireImage/Getty Images, p. 46.

Cover Photo: Pieter Mazel/Sunshine/Retna Ltd, USA.

CONTENTS

TOMORROW THE WORLD

1

On July 4, 1976, the United States celebrated an important birthday— the two hundredth anniversary of the Declaration of Independence, when the Founding Fathers proclaimed the new country's freedom from England. The whole nation was drenched in red, white, and blue for the firework-filled bicentennial parties.

But if the Fourth of July celebrates the shot heard 'round the world and the start of the American Revolution, New York punk-rock band the Ramones were in England on the bicentennial to deliver an explosive blast of sound that would revolutionize rock and roll.

The band's self-titled debut album had just been released. During that trip, the Ramones played a pair of London shows—one at a large venue called the Roundhouse on July 4 and one in a small club called Dingwall's the following night. The gigs were the two-year-old band's first shows outside the United States. The Ramones played short, catchy, and simple songs with volatile energy, creating a wall of sound unlike anything the audiences had heard before. Members of the Clash, the Sex Pistols, and other future legends of British music were in the audience. With those shows, the Ramones helped change the course of musical history by inspiring those aspiring rockers to get out there and start bands.

Clash frontman Joe Strummer explained: "If that Ramones record hadn't existed I don't know that we could have built a scene here, because it fulfilled a vital gap, if you like, between the death of the old pub-rocking scene and the advent of punk."[1]

Strummer was blown away by the Ramones' live show. "It was like white heat because of the constant barrage of the tunes. You couldn't put a cigarette paper between one tune ending and the next beginning," he said.[2]

The Ramones are considered by many to be the founding fathers of punk rock—a high-energy, loud, and fast style of music that stripped rock and roll of excess ornamentation and returned it to its raw roots. Strummer called them "the daddy punk rock group of all time."[3] With their blistering tempos and stripped-down musical skills, the Ramones inspired generations of youths to pick up instruments and start bands of their own. The band's streetwise fashion of leather jackets, T-shirts, ripped jeans, and sneakers was accessible to the masses, and eventually their look became something of a punk-rock uniform.

Ramones manager Danny Fields said the date of the first British show was appropriate, "because here it was the two hundredth anniversary of our freedom from Great Britain, and we were bringing Great Britain this gift that was going to forever disrupt their sensibilities."[4]

The four founding members of the Ramones—singer Joey Ramone, guitarist Johnny Ramone, bassist Dee Dee Ramone, and drummer Tommy Ramone—played the middle slot on the bill, between the American band the Flamin' Groovies and new British band the Stranglers. It was the "hottest, steamiest, dirtiest night of the year" and the Roundhouse was a "swampy sweat box," wrote Max Bell in the British music magazine *NME*.[5]

Bell didn't recognize the historical significance of the show at the time, calling the Ramones "absolutely hilarious," and "closer to a comedy routine than a rock group."[6]

"They succeed in dividing opinion into believers and open ridicule," Bell wrote. "Thing about The Ramones is you either take them in the intended spirit, or you go home."[7]

In an interview, Bell portrayed the band members as

stupid and asked manager Fields why he ever agreed to manage the band. Fields said: "After five seconds I knew I was in the presence of something original. They will be playing in big places soon. Maybe a lot of people hate it but a lot of people love it and those people are going to make them big."[8]

But if Bell wasn't impressed with the band members, he did understand that he was witnessing something new.

"The Ramones don't take the realities of the electronic medium into account; their idea of playing is to plug in with the amps juiced to maximum level and don't let nothin' come in the way of their fingers and your ears," wrote Bell. "They perform so it hurts. Ramone rock forbids the audience to pass pleasantries while it goes down. In return Johnny Ramone leaves the stage with gore-soaked hands most nights, flesh cut to ribbons for the sake of taking your lobes somewhere they were never intended to go."[9]

Writer Mat Snow was also at the Roundhouse and was impressed. "None of us had ever seen anything like it—and when Dee Dee split his thumb open on a bass string, spurting blood all over his white Fender Precision and Prince Charles T-shirt, we knew the Ramones were rock 'n' roll maniacs in the grand old style."[10]

For singer Joey Ramone, the scene the band found in England was just as exciting. "England was like a freak show, a circus, with different-coloured hair and all. It was great, but kinda crazy," Joey said. "That was the beginning of the world

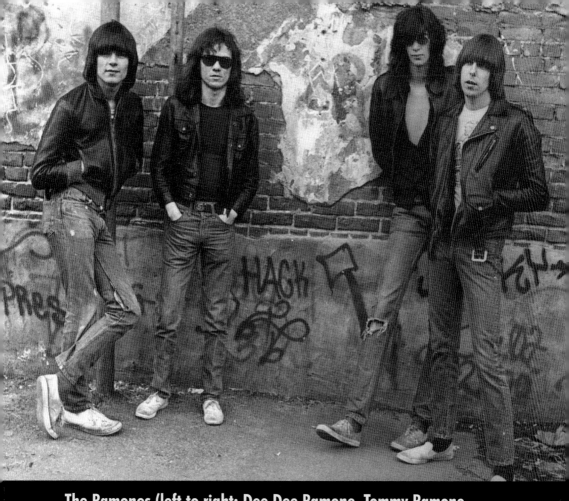

The Ramones (left to right: Dee Dee Ramone, Tommy Ramone,

explosion in England—and then the world changed. *Everything* changed. It wasn't just the music. There was a whole new philosophy and attitude. Everything changed drastically for the better. . . . We put the spirit and guts back into rock 'n' roll."[11]

Chrissie Hynde of the Pretenders recalled, "I was trying to get a band together when I saw them at the Roundhouse. The punk scene was very closely knit and anti-everything. The Ramones were the only 'outside' band that everyone looked up to."[12]

Fields said during that first visit to London, the Ramones advised future members of the Clash Paul Simonon and Mick Jones to get out and start playing. "Paul and Mick weren't in the Clash yet, but they were starting it," Fields said. "They were afraid to play until they saw the Ramones. I mean, Paul and Mick told the Ramones, 'Now that we've seen you, we're gonna be a band.' . . . Basically the Ramones said to them, which they said to countless other bands, 'You don't have to get better, just get out there, you're as good as you are. Don't wait till you're better, how are you ever gonna know? Just go out there and do it."[13]

Getting out there and doing it is what the Ramones did best. Even though the band members frequently feuded with one another and sometimes weren't even on speaking terms, the Ramones stayed together for twenty-two years. In that time, they played 2,263 concerts and released twenty-one studio and live albums. A Ramones T-shirt endures as a badge of coolness for people who may have never even heard the band. And while they never sold many albums or had a hit single, their influence is immense—from garage bands all over the world to major sporting events, where the "Hey Ho Let's Go!" chant from the song "Blitzkrieg Bop" has become ever-present. The word *blitzkrieg* is a German word that means "lightning war," and it was an accurate description of the band's powerful attack.

"They influenced so many people," said Pearl Jam singer Eddie Vedder. "They showed them that they too could do it. The simplicity showed them that they could end up on stage and play in that way."[14]

Metallica guitarist Kirk Hammett agreed, saying, "They showed that anyone, and I mean anyone, can join a rock 'n' roll band. It doesn't really matter what you look like, it's all about what you sound like and what your attitude is."[15]

When he was presenting the Ramones with MTV's Lifetime Achievement Award during the Video Music Awards in 2001, U2 lead singer Bono said, "New York City has given us a lot of things, but the best thing it ever gave us was a punk rock group called the Ramones, without whom a lot of people would never have gotten started—certainly us."[16]

The Ramones have a surprisingly important legacy for a band whose music seems so simple. Joey Ramone explained, "[B]asically what we did was we stripped it down right to the bone and we disassembled it and reassembled it and put all the excitement and fun and spirit, raw energy and raw emotion and guts and attitude back into it."[17]

One of the reasons why many people are so devoted to the Ramones is the band's devotion to its fans.

"Over the years, when fans watched the Ramones play, we always knew they did it for us. They never wavered; they never betrayed our faith," wrote Donna Gaines in the liner notes to the reissue of the groundbreaking first Ramones album. "And their influence has been far-reaching. With their stripped-down streetwise anti-look, combined with speed-pop raw aggression and darkly funny lyrics, the Ramones have informed music genres from new wave to hardcore, speed metal, and thrash."[18]

The story of the Ramones begins in the Forest Hills section of Queens, New York, where the founding members all knew firsthand what it was like to be misfits and outcasts— and understood the power of rock and roll to help relieve that teenage boredom and isolation.

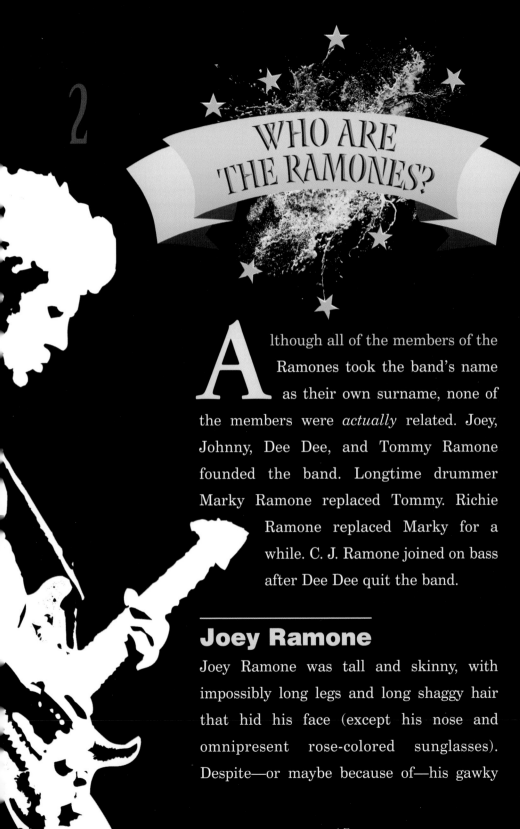

WHO ARE THE RAMONES?

Although all of the members of the Ramones took the band's name as their own surname, none of the members were *actually* related. Joey, Johnny, Dee Dee, and Tommy Ramone founded the band. Longtime drummer Marky Ramone replaced Tommy. Richie Ramone replaced Marky for a while. C. J. Ramone joined on bass after Dee Dee quit the band.

Joey Ramone

Joey Ramone was tall and skinny, with impossibly long legs and long shaggy hair that hid his face (except his nose and omnipresent rose-colored sunglasses). Despite—or maybe because of—his gawky and gangly appearance, Joey made the perfect rock-and-roll frontman.

Joey Ramone was born Jeffrey Hyman on May 19, 1951, in Forest Hills. His parents divorced when he was young. Joey's younger brother, Mickey Leigh, described an environment where they felt like outsiders from a young age—and responded with a sense of humor.

"The humor was inherent to Forest Hills, a Jewish neighborhood, and to the small circle of rejects and misfits that we were," Leigh explained. "We were always on the outside, rejected by the girls—not by all girls, but by the pretty ones, who preferred guys with cars. Our protective shell was to shock people."[1]

Joey, in particular, felt isolated. "I spent a lot of time by myself," he said. "Music was my salvation."[2]

Joey's early influences included Del Shannon, Phil Spector, the Beatles, Rolling Stones, Shangri-Las, Kinks, Beach Boys, and the Who.[3] Later on, he got into glam rock. Glam, short for "glamour," was an outrageous style of rock and roll that featured men wearing makeup and feminine clothes. "I was definitely a rock fan and I was really into record collecting, but I was maybe into like, more extreme things, like Slade and T. Rex and Gary Glitter and all that stuff."[4]

For Joey, rock music helped him get past his feelings of being weird.

"Rock 'n' roll was a savior. It gave you the sense of being

Joey Ramone in 1976

an individual. It was something *you* had—nobody else but you," Joey said. "I remember my father getting me a radio that you hooked on the window sill and then listened to with an earphone. I used to listen to it under the covers and get caught."[5]

Joey suffered from a condition known as obsessive-compulsive disorder (OCD). OCD is an anxiety disorder, and people who suffer from it have recurrent, unwanted thoughts and often engage in repetitive behaviors in the hopes of making those thoughts go away. Those ritual behaviors—like handwashing, counting, repeatedly checking things, or cleaning—only provide temporary relief, and not performing the rituals increases the anxiety.[6]

Joey had many rituals he felt compelled to perform because of OCD. He would touch things repeatedly or do certain actions over and over.

"He couldn't go in and out of the door. He had to close the door 100 times. He had to run up and downstairs, crossing streets over and over, on and off corners," said Ramones long-time tour manager Monte Melnick.[7]

Along with his OCD, Joey had other difficulties to overcome.

"The projections for him from childhood were not good," said Joey's mother, Charlotte Lesher. "The teachers said 'His eyes are bad, he's not reading well.' He was a slow student, but they didn't think about his basic intelligence. He was highly intelligent and very, very creative. They didn't even look at that side of him."[8]

Later in his career, Joey also developed a problem with alcohol and cocaine abuse, but he stopped after he fell offstage in 1990. Melnick said, "After that fall, he decided to stop drinking, cut out the drugs and seek the healthy life. He never really took care of himself until after he kicked alcohol."[9]

Johnny Ramone

Of the four founding members of the Ramones, only Joey and Johnny stayed with the band for its entire history. With his pudding-bowl haircut and jackhammer downstroke guitar style, Johnny used his instrument like a weapon. If Joey was the sensitive heart of the Ramones, Johnny was the band's nerve center whose business sense and military-like demeanor helped keep the band on track.

Johnny was born John Cummings on October 8, 1948, on Long Island (although many biographies say he was born in 1951) to a construction-worker father and a waitress mother.[10]

From a very early age, Johnny was attracted to rock-and-roll music—especially after he saw one of rock's originators cause a ruckus on television. Elvis Presley was a rock pioneer and is often called the "King of Rock and Roll." Ed Sullivan hosted one of the most popular shows on television in the 1950s and 1960s, and when Elvis performed on the show

Johnny Ramone in 1979

in 1956, the television camera showed him only from the waist up, to hide his wild hip-shaking dancing, which some thought was indecent.[11]

"All I ever wanted to do was be a rock star since I was four and I saw Elvis on the Ed Sullivan show when they banned the TV station from showing shots of him below the waist," Johnny said.[12]

Johnny had a rough time as a teenager trying to figure out what he wanted to do with his life. He began to get involved with drugs and crime. "The late teens are a very big period for kids, when you don't know what to do with yourself, when there's pressure to go to college and get a job." He continued, "It's a crisis time, especially if you don't really enjoy school and aren't good at it. For me those years were basically delinquent. Then all of a sudden one day, I was walking down the block and it hit me like a voice from above: What am I going to do with my life? Is this what I'm here for—to be delinquent? So I stopped doing anything that was wrong—no more drinking, drugs or anything bad, which I'd been doing all day long, every minute of the day."[13]

Johnny was an avid baseball fan—particularly of the New York Yankees. But his sense of rebellion prevented him from playing the sport he loved. "I've wanted to be a baseball player since I was five, but to be on the high school team you had to get a haircut, and even then I couldn't take any sort of discipline," he said.[14]

Dee Dee Ramone

Bassist Dee Dee Ramone was in many ways the most tortured member of the Ramones, and he was responsible for some of the band's best—and darkest—songs. Dee Dee was born Douglas Colvin on September 18, 1952, in Virginia. His mother was from Germany, and his father served in the U.S. Army. Dee Dee's family lived a nomadic military life, splitting time between army bases in the United States and Germany. In his autobiography, Dee Dee described his mother as "a drunken nut job" and his father as a "weak, selfish drunk."[15]

"My father was constantly beating on me, yelling at me, and blaming me for everything. I started developing a really low self-esteem," Dee Dee wrote.[16]

Because of the abuse he suffered at home and the isolation that comes from moving from place to place, Dee Dee began to develop a rebellious streak. "Rebels were a lot cooler to me than squares," he wrote. "My parents seemed like a continual drag. I could never forgive them for what was going on at home."[17]

With such a bleak home life, Dee Dee turned to music. "Somehow, even at the age of twelve, I knew I was a loser. I couldn't see a future for myself," he wrote. "Then I heard the Beatles for the first time. I got my first transistor radio, a

Dee Dee Ramone in 1977

Beatle haircut and a Beatle suit. . . . I identified with these new rock and roll songs that were played on Radio Luxembourg, the pirate station that broadcast from the English Channel."[18]

Unfortunately, Dee Dee also discovered drugs around the same time, beginning a lifelong struggle with substance abuse—particularly heroin. His addictions made him unpredictable. "A lot of Dee Dee's behavior was caused by his drug use," Tommy said. "He was the type of person you couldn't give a drink to because he'd drink till he passed out. It was the same with the drugs. He used to do a lot of drugs and some of his problems might have been due to actual damage from years and years of abusing drugs."[19]

Dee Dee was well-known for his heroin addiction. He wrote a notorious song about heroin called "Chinese Rocks," and that solidified his image as an addict, even when he tried to stop using drugs. "I feel like I became some kind of heroin guru," Dee Dee said.[20]

Tommy Ramone

Tommy Ramone was born Tommy Erdelyi in Budapest, Hungary, on January 29, 1952. His family moved to the United States in 1956. His early years in Hungary were spent under a Communist government at the height of the cold war. Communism is a system of government that is opposed to private wealth and where a single political party has total control of the country. During that time, the countries in the eastern part of Europe were Communist, and there was a conflict between the Communist countries in the east and the democratic countries of the west (like the United States). That conflict involved military buildups but not actual violence, and so it was referred to as the cold war.

"It was a very restrictive regime, you didn't hear too much Western music," he said. "I remember the early stages of rock 'n' roll, how much it excited me—even as a young kid I was into dressing cool, into wearing a certain type of shoes. It was nice there, except for the political regime. One of the first records I had was a score to a Hungarian movie, with a rock beat to it, making fun of America."[21]

He became friends with Johnny when they were students at Forest Hills High School. "I met Johnny in the cafeteria in my first year of high school. Our connection was music," Tommy said.[22]

Before they were in the Ramones, Johnny and Tommy played in a band called Tangerine Puppets. That band played songs by rock pioneers like Bo Diddley and the Rolling Stones, as well as early garage bands like Count Five and the Shadows of Knight. That band's brutal performing style was a preview of the Ramones' aggressive attack.

"Johnny would have his guitar slung really high and dive around wildly, using it like a machine gun," Tommy said. "One day we played at the high school and we were hopping around,

Tommy
Ramone
in 1976

and Johnny ran into a girl with his guitar and we got banned from school."[23]

After high school, Tommy continued working as a musician. He worked as a recording engineer at a studio called the Record Plant in New York, including work on a session with legendary guitarist Jimi Hendrix.[24]

Tommy and fellow Forest Hills resident Monte Melnick founded Performance Studios, which was a rehearsal and recording space in Manhattan. "We built that place by hand, designed it and everything," Melnick said. "We had a main stage, a separate booth with a glass wall for a four-track recorder, a rehearsal studio, offices and a lobby. We provided much of the gear ourselves, so we got all the free studio time we wanted in return."[25]

Eventually, Performance Studios was where the Ramones first got together as a band, and Melnick went on to be the Ramones' road manager.

Marky Ramone

Marky Ramone was born Marc Bell on July 15, 1956, in Brooklyn and grew up in the tough, gang-infested neighborhood of Flatbush. His father was a longshoreman, and his mother ran the music library at Brooklyn College.[26]

Marky's mother is the one who introduced him to Beatles drummer Ringo Starr. "There was always music around," Marky said. "When I was eight, my mother told me to come in and watch the Beatles on Ed Sullivan—that's what started me off wanting to play drums, Ringo. He kept the beat and had a good sound."[27]

Before joining the Ramones in 1978, he played in a power trio called Dust. He also played drums with Richard Hell and the Voidoids, whose song "The Blank Generation" helped create the blueprint for punk rock.

"I was hanging out in New York City and started getting into the new sounds that were being created, and started playing with Richard Hell and the Voidoids on their debut album," Marky said.[28]

C. J. Ramone

When founding member Dee Dee left the Ramones, many thought they wouldn't be able to continue. But after holding auditions, bassist C. J. Ramone was hired. C. J. was born Christopher Joseph Ward in Queens on October 8, 1965. His first instrument was the drums. "When I was young, I played drums but they must've been too noisy, because I came home one day and they were gone," he said.[29]

He started playing bass when he was thirteen years old. He grew up listening to classic rock like Neil Young and Creedence Clearwater Revival, as well as heavy metal bands like Judas Priest and Iron Maiden. He also was a big Ramones fan.[30]

"I liked the Ramones because of the incredible amount of

energy that came off the stage—the choreography, and of course the songs. The show was non-stop. Joey had a real strong presence, and Dee Dee and Johnny were in constant motion," he said.[31]

Richie Ramone

Drummer Richie Ramone—born Richard Reinhardt on August 11, 1957—joined the Ramones in 1983 and stayed through 1987. Richie was inspired to play drums by jazz legend Buddy Rich. "I've been drumming since I was 4 years old," he said. "The drummer is the ultimate driver of an orchestra—I don't care what anyone says."[32]

Richie had a strict upbringing in New Jersey and didn't always get along with his parents. "They wanted to send me to West Point," he said. "One of those schools where they want to send you away to become a better kid."[33]

He left home when he was seventeen, moving to New York and playing with the band Velveteen before joining the Ramones.[34]

3

HEY HO LET'S GO!

The story of the Ramones began in the Forest Hills neighborhood of Queens, New York, where the four founding members of the band grew up. "Forest Hills is one of those neighborhoods which is a subway ride to and from Manhattan," wrote Dee Dee. "It is a nicely groomed neighborhood with lots of Coupe deVilles and Lincolns parked on the street. All the buildings are the same redbrick color and chewing-gum-colored sidewalks snake through the area. There are little fringes of grass hugging the buildings where the dogs go to the bathroom. In the mornings, the janitors would burn the trash in incinerators and a thick gray smoke would pour out of the chimneys."[1]

All four future Ramones lived in the same apartment complex in Forest Hills and went to Forest Hills High School.[2] High school was a tough time for them all—none of them seemed to fit in.

"People who join a band like the Ramones don't come from stable backgrounds, because it's not that civilized an art form. Punk rock comes from angry kids who feel like being creative," Dee Dee wrote. "When you're sixteen years old, angry and bored, you have to be very creative to stir up some excitement."[3]

Music was a unifying force. The future Ramones bonded over Detroit bands like the MC5 and the Stooges, which featured frontman Iggy Pop, who many consider to be the first punk rocker. Many consider those two bands to be direct ancestors of punk rock.

"When I first told John that the Stooges were my favorite group, he said he liked them also," Dee Dee wrote. "I couldn't believe it. Someone else in Forest Hills liked the Stooges besides me. It was like a miracle. To me, the Stooges were the most real rock 'n' roll band around. They were the best. . . . They were very, very creepy."[4]

Along with the MC5 and the Stooges, a group called the New York Dolls was massively influential on the Ramones and other punk rockers. The Dolls dressed up in flamboyant women's outfits and played a kind of stripped-down rock

MC5 was one of the bands that the Ramones found influential.

music that placed a greater emphasis on energy than it did on polish. The Dolls played a music called "glam" or "glitter."

The Dolls provided the spark of inspiration for the Ramones. "We saw them, and realized that they were a great band and that they really didn't play well at all. So maybe we didn't need to play guitar twenty years to play rock 'n' roll—which was never what rock 'n' roll was about," Johnny said.[5]

The Ramones' music was a reaction to the rock music of the time. Bands like Yes and Emerson Lake and Palmer were releasing long, keyboard-drenched albums that featured flashy musical technique and fanciful lyrics. Bands were spending increasing amounts of time—and money—in the studio making their albums. At the beginning of 1974, *Rolling Stone* magazine named the best artists of the previous year. The magazine honored Southern rock group the Allman Brothers as band of the year. The Allman Brothers were known for long bluesy jams with lots of fiery guitar solos. The trend of the year was "Third World music," which referred to Jamaican reggae music and a type of dance music called "disco." Disco music featured a prominent, repetitive beat and was meant for flowing dancing, and the music inspired glitzy fashions. Mellow rockers Elton John and Bette Midler were named rock stars of the year by the magazine.[6]

Along with a lack of energy in rock music, life in the United States was difficult when the Ramones formed. A *Rolling Stone* "World News Roundup" in September 1973 gives a good snapshot of life in the United States around the time the Ramones got together. The collection of articles talked about shortages of beef and gasoline. Gas stations cut their hours and long lines formed waiting to fill up. According to one writer in Denver, "Most drivers in the area have been trying to keep a full tank, searching out a gas station whenever the needle drops to the halfway mark." A political survey showed that 68 percent of people polled viewed President Richard M. Nixon unfavorably.[7]

In 1974, a wiretapping scandal known as Watergate forced Nixon to resign (the first American president to do so). The long, bloody, and controversial Vietnam War was coming to an end—the last American troops would leave in 1975.

Tommy was already working in the music business with Performance Studio, and he thought his old friends from Forest Hills would make an interesting band.

"I saw how exciting [the New York Dolls] were despite the fact that they weren't really virtuoso musicians," Tommy said. "The idea hit me—I knew these great kids from Queens who would make a great band because they were so unusual."[8]

Tommy brought them together to practice at his rehearsal studio as a band.

"Johnny Ramone and I really had no intention of ever playing in groups again. We both had bitter experiences of other groups we had been in before the Ramones started," Dee Dee wrote.[9]

But they, like Tommy, were impressed with the New York Dolls, and "after the Dolls broke up, there were still a bunch of creeps who needed a scene," Dee Dee wrote.[10]

Joey had been singing with a glitter band called Sniper under the name Jeff Starship. Joey's brother, Mickey Leigh, said, "Joey really got into the glitter thing. He was stealing all my mother's jewelry, her clothes, her makeup, and her scarves, which created even more fights between them. She would flip out when she saw all her clothes were missing."[11]

At first, Tommy wasn't in the band, he was merely advising them. Joey played drums and Dee Dee played bass and sang. There were just two problems—Dee Dee couldn't play and sing at the same time, and Joey wasn't a very good drummer. Tommy suggested that Joey take over lead singing duties.

"We put an ad in the paper and auditioned drummers," Tommy said. "I didn't know how to play drums, but I'd sit down and show them how to play these songs. They couldn't get it. So then the guys started saying 'Why don't *you* try playing drums?' I tried it for fun and it clicked somehow."[12]

The idea for the band's name came from Dee Dee, who was inspired by a false name Paul McCartney used in the early days of the Beatles' career. "Dee Dee started calling himself Dee Dee Ramone," Joey said. "He was a Paul McCartney fan.

When Paul McCartney would check into a hotel, he'd use the alias of 'Ramone.' Paul Ramone. Before the Ramones were even a band, Dee Dee was using that name."[13]

After nearly nine months of practice, the Ramones were looking for a place to play. They found it in a grimy nightclub called CBGB's, which would become the center of the New York punk universe. Located on New York's Lower East Side, the area around CBGB's was rough and frightening—a reflection of the difficulties in New York City during that era.

"The Lower East Side was really scary. It was bombed out," said *Punk* magazine cofounder Legs McNeil, who was part of the same scene. "There were burned-out buildings that they just left up that looked like these facades of destroyed ruins in Germany at the end of World War II."[14]

Arturo Vega, the Ramones' art director, noted: "It was a part of town that was considered very undesirable. It was crime-ridden. It was full of drug dealers and drug users. And we liked it that way."[15]

Blondie guitarist Chris Stein said, "It was great. It was like the Wild West. And it didn't cost anything to . . . live here."[16]

The club, founded by a man named Hilly Kristal, opened in December 1973. The full name—CBGB & OMFUG—was an abbreviation for the kind of music he hoped to book:

Hilly Kristal opened CBGB's in the early 1970s.

"Country, Bluegrass, Blues and Other Music For Uplifting Gourmandizers [lovers of good food and drink]."[17]

"There was no real venue in 1973 for people like us," said Patti Smith, who was one of many artists who played at CBGB's in the early days. "We didn't fit into the cabarets or the folk clubs. Hilly wanted the people that nobody else wanted. He wanted us."[18]

There was a reason why the club was the source of so much great music. Photographer Bob Gruen said, "Hilly only had one rule about bands in CBGB's. It was that they had to write their own songs. At that time, most bands up until then had played cover songs. So it was always new, it was always interesting, it was always very different. So one night it could be some crazy loud people, the next night it could be some experimental jazz people, the next night it was somebody with a fiddle and a tuba, the next night it could be five loud guitars. You never knew what to expect."[19]

Because of Hilly's directive, many famous and ground-breaking bands came out of the CBGB's scene, including Blondie, Talking Heads, Patti Smith, Television, Richard Hell and the Voidoids, the Heartbreakers, and the Dead Boys.

Kristal explained his policy in an interview with the *New York Times* in 1977. "I started hiring groups, and eventually I began stimulating things by insisting on original material and creativity," he said. "I still don't look particularly for fine tech-nique or great showmanship. I just look for something in the music, some feeling that a group is expressing in a slightly different way."[20]

Talking Heads keyboard player Jerry Harrison said: "It was so *nurturing*, even by its mere shape. It's a long, narrow room, so even if there's only 20 people there, they'll be at the front so it at least feels like there's an audience. And if you didn't like a band, you could just go to the bar at the back or even out on the sidewalk and talk with your friends, and move upfront for someone you really wanted to see. Hilly Kristal made it feel like our club, and thus allowed the scene to happen."[21]

Singer and bassist Richard Hell said the CBGB's scene was small, but it was filled with creative people. "We were the most intense thing going on in the world for sure—just full of life and ideas," he said. "But at the same time, it was a dead end little nowhere joint that was only known to a really devoted and intense 300 or 400 people in New York who had these very specific, extreme tastes."[22]

The Ramones played CBGB's for the first time in August 1974. Video clips from a performance there a month later are rough, but show the kernel of what the Ramones would become. Joey pranced about like a glam rocker and Johnny was shirtless underneath his Stooges-styled leather jacket. Band members would make mistakes and fight between songs over what to play next.

"The first time they played it was terrible," said Hilly

Kristal. "They didn't get good for a few months. But when they did, they played 20 songs in 17 minutes without stopping and that caused a sensation."[23]

One of the things that made the Ramones distinctive was the fact that their songs were catchy and melodic pop songs at the core. From the very beginning, the Ramones drew inspiration from their dissatisfaction with the sounds they were hearing on the radio. That frustration with mainstream music has always been a big motivator for punk rock.

"We used to sit around and listen to the radio and not hear anything like the stuff we like," Tommy told writer Alan Betrock in 1975. "So we decided to play it ourselves."[24]

Right from the get-go, the Ramones began earning a reputation for vigorous performances. Writing in the *Soho Weekly News*, Betrock described the band as "a total energy blast."[25] His description of an early Ramones show sounds like a show from any point in the band's career. "The group does song after song with hardly a word spoken. The longest lapse between each song is 13 seconds," Betrock wrote. "Each tune is built on a few chopping, grinding chords, heavily churned out by Johnny Ramone. Dee Dee and Tommy Ramone form this unified rhythm section which seems devoted to capturing the three best riffs in rock and utilizing them over and over again. Joey Ramone, the young broomstick of a lead singer tries to get the lyrics out over the surge, while at the same time pushing his specs back on to his face."[26]

Betrock described the band's music as "rock and roll the way it was meant to be played, not with boogie or pretense, but just straight freshness and intense energy. Sort of out of the garages and onto the stages again."[27]

Tommy had a comic response when asked why the Ramones played so fast, saying: "We play short songs and short sets for people who don't have a lot of spare time."[28]

At the end of 1974, the Ramones went into the studio and recorded a demo of fifteen songs over eight hours. "It was a lot of fun," Tommy said. "It felt like we were making important music. We knew we didn't sound like anyone else. It was funny and smart and good."[29]

The scene around CBGB's was heating up, but it didn't translate into a record deal right away. "We were playing CBGB three nights every three weeks, and drawing 600 people a night," Johnny said. "But nobody was interested in signing us."[30]

Finally, the band played an audition for Seymour Stein, founder of Sire Records. He was blown away by their half-hour set. "It was like I put my hand in a light socket while standing in a bathtub," Stein remembered. "I was electrified."[31]

The band's self-titled first album was released in July 1976. The album was recorded cheaply—for $6,400—during seventeen days at a studio called Plaza Sound in the famed

Radio City Music Hall. The album's fourteen tracks clock in at less than twenty-nine minutes.[32]

The album kicked off with one of the Ramones' most famous songs, "Blitzkrieg Bop," and its familiar chant of "Hey Ho Let's Go!"

"It's an ode to the rock 'n' roll fan," Tommy said. "It's about having a good time at a music show, the excitement of seeing your favorite band. It's about fans and bands, a love letter to the fans."[33]

Nowadays, many people recognize *Ramones* as one of the greatest rock albums of all time. When it was first released, the album received some high critical praise in the music press. Kris Needs in *ZigZag* wrote:

> It only lasts 28 minutes—but then if you travel at double the speed, you get there in half the time. And there's no guitar solos, either, just Johnny Ramone's rampaging block-chord power-riffing, which threatens to burn holes in the speakers. Joey Ramone's vocals are a cross between New York Street jive and a mid-'60s British pop singer. Dunno how affected the accent is, but once you get used to it, it's pretty amusing, missed syllables and all. The mutant vocals and ultra-simplicity of the music and the lyrics do take some getting used to, but once you get past the curiosity stage, the effect can be shattering, especially at high volume.[34]

Other positive reviews included:

- "Recapturing the essence of rock," *Hollywood Daily Variety.*
- "There hasn't been an album in five years as strong or invigorating as this. It's as if a hydrogen bomb hit Herman's Hermits," Howard Wuelfing, *Washington Times.*
- "The best young rock and roll band in the known universe," Wayne Robbins, *Newsday.*

But not all the critics understood the Ramones' music—there were many negative reviews as well.

- "Humorless poor taste performed by the missing links of rock and roll," Ken Wilson, *Hollywood Press.*
- "Uniquely repulsive. Not a scrap of taste. The stuff of which bad myths are made," Paul McGrath, *Toronto Globe & Mail.*
- "They don't waste their time—they waste yours," Stephen Ford, *Detroit News.*
- "El Stinko garbage of the worst kind," *Dayton Journal Herald.*
- "Rotten. No musical promise or any cultural advances or redeeming social values. They deserve to be ignored," Jim Girard, *Cleveland Scene.*[35]

Sire Records collected snippets from the good and bad

reviews for an ad in support of the Ramones' second album, *Leave Home*. The album was recorded at Sundragon Studios in Manhattan and released in April 1977. Tommy described the album as "heavier, more melodic, with more bite."[36]

"That was our mood—insane pop songs with lyrics inspired by cheesy slasher and horror flicks, with a happy-go-lucky feel to it," Tommy said.[37]

While many considered the Ramones' act to be dumbed-down, some believed that they were a great example of a style of art known as "minimalism." Minimalism is a movement in art and music where everything that is unnecessary is stripped away, leaving just the pure essence.

Writer Mick Farren made that argument in the *NME*. He wrote: "'I wanna' is probably the most important phrase in the whole limited minimalist vocabulary. The Ramones have made it a means to express just about any human desire or emotion. By telling the listener what they wanna do, wanna be, wanna have or what they wanna get rid of, they've just about rendered any more elaborate lyrics obsolete."[38]

Over the band's career, the Ramones wrote many songs with lyrics that contained the words "I wanna" or "I don't wanna." Among the things the Ramones don't wanna do:

- go down to the basement
- get involved with you
- walk around with you
- grow up

- live this life anymore
- be learned or tamed
- be buried in a pet cemetery

On the other hand, the Ramones do wanna:

- be well
- be sedated
- be your boyfriend
- live
- get shock treatment

Donna Gaines wrote in a CD reissue of the album that "*Leave Home* showcases the Ramones' special gift for infusing everyday life experience with dark humor, street smarts, and pop savvy, then elevating it to higher ground. Lurking underneath each pop ditty was a serious subtext, a treatise on universal themes such as human alienation, boredom and fear. These feelings are powerful and overwhelming, especially for kids."[39]

Leave Home featured another classic Ramones song called "Pinhead." That song began with the chant "Gabba Gabba / We accept you / We accept you / One of us" and ended with a chant of "Gabba Gabba Hey." That song was a climax of Ramones concerts—Joey would haul out a giant sign that said "Gabba Gabba Hey" and the crowd would chant along.

That chant was inspired by a 1932 film called *Freaks*, directed by Tod Browning. The film featured real carnival

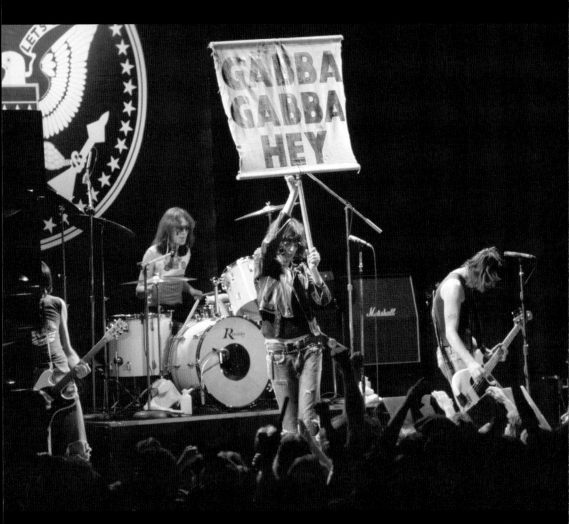

Joey Ramone holds up a "Gabba Gabba Hey" sign at a concert in 1978.

sideshow performers—people with physical disabilities who were exhibited to the public as oddities. At one point, the "freaks" chant "Gooble Gobble Gooble Gobble / We accept you we accept you / One of us, One of us." That scene seemed to resonate with the Ramones, who felt like misfits growing up. "I saw that movie ten times, it's one of our biggest inspirations," Johnny said.[40]

The record received positive reviews in the music press. "The Ramones are as direct and witty as before. They've also lost just a pinch of their studied rawness: whether this is a sign of maturity or sellout is a matter of debate," wrote Ken Tucker in *Rolling Stone*. "The Ramones make rousing music and damn good jokes, but they're in a bit of a bind: the hard rock of this group is so pure it may be perceived as a freak novelty by a lot of people."[41]

In the *Village Voice,* Robert Christgau wrote: "People who consider this a one-joke act aren't going to change their minds now. People who love the joke for its power, wit, and economy will be happy to hear it twice."[42]

In *ZigZag,* reviewer Kris Needs wrote that *Leave Home* was a step forward for the Ramones. "Sure it's basically the same ingredients: the white-hot, pummelling guitar and simple not-as-dumb-as-they-look lyrics, delivered with deadpan vocals," Needs wrote. "But on this album there's something extra . . . more refinements, I s'pose. Catchier tunes, subtly effective production touches, varying tempos, other influences . . . it's sure no retread job."[43]

By 1977, the music scene seemed ready for change. Elvis Presley died in August of that year. The music on the radio was increasingly slick and highly produced. Top albums that year included Meat Loaf's *Bat Out of Hell,* Fleetwood Mac's *Rumours,* and the Eagles' *Hotel California.* Disco had become even more popular, as shown in the following year's popular movie *Saturday Night Fever.* Even rock-and-roll bands like KISS, the Rolling Stones, and the Grateful Dead put out disco records. In many ways, the punk scene was a reaction to those trends.

So 1977 seemed to hold a lot of promise for the punk-rock bands at CBGB's. Blondie's song "In the Flesh" was an unexpected number one in Australia. "All of a sudden, everybody wanted to sign punk bands," said Richard Gottehrer, cofounder of Sire Records. "[The year] 1977 is the seminal year. It opened up a whole new world of music to people, and it opened the eyes of an industry that needed the new Elvis. And then comes along this collection of people in this small venue, and they're creating change."[44]

Arturo Vega remembered, "[The year] '77 was actually a landmark year for CBGB. The punk scene gets a lot of attention, not only in the local press or the New York press or the American press, but the world press came to CBGB right away. We had as many as 600 people inside CBGB for a

Ramones show. Somehow you used to see like two or three layers of people—people standing on the ground, then people standing on chairs and people standing on the railings. So it's like, you know, the Bowery is on fire."[45]

New York wasn't the only place experiencing a punk-rock explosion. England's punk bands—most notably the Sex Pistols and the Clash—were gaining a lot of attention in London.

As far as Joey was concerned, the Ramones and the Sex Pistols seemed poised to take on the world. "We kinda felt us and the Sex Pistols would become almost like the Beatles and the Stones of the '60s—we were the new revolution," Joey said.[46]

The third Ramones album—and the second released in 1977—was called *Rocket to Russia*. Again it was filled with classic Ramones songs, including "Rockaway Beach." Written by Dee Dee, the song sounds like a souped-up Beach Boys song, with all-American lyrics like "chewing out a rhythm on my bubblegum." In reality, though it's an example of how the Ramones could find beauty in ugly places, according to Legs McNeil.

"Rockaway Beach is the band's anthem to every juvenile delinquent's ultimate summer beach party," wrote McNeil, describing a scene where there were "crowds of vicious girls in bikinis and—I swear—*high heels*, drinking tallboys

The Sex Pistols received a lot of attention in the late 1970s.

of beer out of little brown paper bags, waiting to get into the next fight."[47]

"The real Rockaway Beach was never so 'bouncy' and innocent as the Ramones' song," McNeil wrote. "But that's what's so cool about it—and revolutionary. The simplicity . . . was this: Let's take everything . . . miserable about our lives and celebrate it!"[48]

The song "Sheena Is a Punk Rocker" reached number eighty-one on the *Billboard* singles. "'Sheena' not only proved that punk could have commercial appeal but also helped give the term *punk* some of its first positive mass exposure," McNeil wrote.[49]

But fate stepped in and kept the Ramones from taking advantage of those successes. First, Joey suffered second- and third-degree burns in Passaic, New Jersey, while he was inhaling steam to clear his sinuses and throat before singing. That injury caused the tour to be canceled, and it cost the Ramones some momentum.[50]

Then, the Sex Pistols from England began getting a lot of attention and turned a lot of people off to punk rock with their antisocial behavior. The band played a short and disastrous American tour before breaking up in early 1978. "Safety pins, razor blades, chopped haircuts, snarling, vomiting—everything that had nothing to do with the

Ramones was suddenly in vogue, and it killed any chance *Rocket to Russia* had of getting any airplay," McNeil wrote.[51]

Joey said the negative publicity surrounding the Sex Pistols turned people off to any punk-rock music, killing the chart potential for "Sheena Is a Punk Rocker."

"The record was doing really well, and then one day on *60 Minutes* was a thing about the Sex Pistols . . . and everybody flipped out and then things changed radically," Joey said. "It really kind of screwed things up for ourselves."[52]

Joey's burns inspired one of the Ramones' most classic songs, "I Wanna Be Sedated." He wrote it New Year's Eve 1977–1978 in London, where the band was playing a show at the Rainbow. Joey told comanager Linda Stein: "Put me in a wheelchair and get me on a plane before I go insane."[53] Those words ended up in the song's chorus.

While they were still working hard, the Ramones' dreams of becoming an overnight sensation were beginning to vanish. Sire Records' Seymour Stein said the disappointing sales of *Rocket to Russia* had a lasting effect on the band. "Warner Bros. had been geared up in all departments, and when *Rocket to Russia* didn't live up to anybody's expectations, the Ramones seemed indelibly stamped in everybody's mind . . . as a cult band that wasn't for everybody," Stein said.[54]

That dissatisfaction—and the frustrating search for smash commercial success—would stay with the Ramones for the rest of their career. In one way, *Rocket to Russia* was the end of an era. The songs recorded on the first three albums were all written before the release of the first album, and they were recorded more or less in the order they were written. "The structures were slightly different by the second album, but there was a natural progression from album to album, and we didn't blow our best fourteen songs on the first album and come back with a weaker second one—which is always what happens with bands," Johnny said.[55]

ROAD TO RUIN

4

By 1978, the Ramones had released three albums and toured nonstop and still hadn't achieved the commercial success they desired. During the next few years, the band would try making changes to its original recipe to achieve that success. They would make a movie, work with different producers, and try to write more poppy tunes. First there was a lineup change.

After *Rocket to Russia*, the pressure of the band's heavy touring schedule led Tommy to quit the Ramones before the band went into the studio to record its next album, *Road to Ruin*.

"We weren't getting along too well by *Road to Ruin* and they were driving me crazy," explains Tommy. "Back in the early days the band got along great. There were problems, but nothing serious. When we went on the road, pretty quickly it got bad. . . . I was on the verge of a nervous breakdown, and they thought this was hilarious. I didn't know it at the time, but I was suffering from depression. So I said I couldn't do it anymore."[1]

New drummer Marky joined the Ramones three weeks before they went into the studio to record *Road to Ruin* in May, and he played his first show with the Ramones in June 1978. "It worked out real well," Tommy said. "Marky liked my playing, and combined my style with his talent."[2]

Tommy stayed on board to coproduce *Road to Ruin,* which was released in September 1978.

The album received mixed reviews. *New York Rocker* reviewer Roy Trakin called *Road to Ruin* "an uneven, sometimes lazy LP," adding that the band "seem as if they are riding the wave rather than anticipating it."[3]

Trakin preferred Tommy's drum style to Marky's, writing: "His light, distinctive, jazz-influenced drumming is sorely missed on *Road to Ruin* as Marky is of the heads-down basher school."[4]

Rolling Stone reviewer Charles M. Young called *Road to Ruin* "a real good album," but not "as funny or as powerful as their debut."[5]

Young particularly noted the growth in Joey's singing. "He achieves a sincerity on *Road to Ruin* that has heretofore

The Ramones in 1977 (left to right: Dee Dee Ramone, Johnny
Ramone, Joey Ramone, and Marky Ramone)

eluded him," Young wrote. "'Needles and Pins,' the old Searchers hit, could have been just a dumb joke. Joey, however, really puts his guts into these antiquated but beautiful lyrics and pulls it off."[6]

In December 1978, the Ramones began work on a film with legendary B-movie producer Roger Corman and director Alan Arkush. The movie *Rock 'n' Roll High School* tells the story of the fictitious Vince Lombardi High School, which is run by a rock-and-roll-hating principal named Miss Togar and her team of repressive hall monitors. Her nemesis was rebellious student and Ramones fan student Riff Randell. The Ramones were the heroes of the movie, with speaking roles and lots of high-energy live performance footage.

Arkush grew up in New Jersey, and he first came up with the idea when he was in high school. "I used to daydream in class all the time, about having go-cart races in the hallway and blowing up the school. And I imagined getting a rock band like the Yardbirds to play there," Arkush said.[7]

Corman's original concept was to make a movie called *Disco High,* but Arkush believed the film needed a more aggressive style of music. "One day he came to me and said, 'Roger, You can't blow up a high school to disco music,'" Corman said.[8]

"Ultimately what the picture was about is how you like

In 1978, the Ramones appeared in a movie, *Rock 'n' Roll High School.*

music because of who you are and what you'd like to be," Arkush said.[9]

The story of *Rock 'n' Roll High School* is "[a] classic confrontation between mindless authority and the rebellious nature of youth," as one of the characters describes it in the film. It is filled with wacky comic gags and rocking live footage of the band.

"It's really nice that the message of the Ramones and the feeling that they give when you watch them is tied up with the movie," Arkush said.[10]

Costar Clint Howard said, "Rock and roll is rebellion with a smile on your face, and that's what Alan delivered with *Rock 'n' Roll High School*."[11]

Much like the Ramones' music, *Rock 'n' Roll High School* wasn't a huge commercial success, but it became a cult hit on college campuses and at late-night showings.

In May 1979, the Ramones began working on their next album with legendary producer Phil Spector. Spector's production style, called the "Wall of Sound," was behind a string of hits in the 1960s for artists like the Ronettes, the Crystals, and the Righteous Brothers. He also worked on the Beatles' last album and produced first solo albums by ex-Beatles John Lennon and George Harrison.

"Though he rarely released records under his name, as a producer Phil Spector has influenced the course of rock and roll more than all but a handful of performers," wrote

Richie Unterberger in the *All Music Guide*. "To an extent that had never been imagined in rock & roll, Spector pumped his records full of orchestration—strings, horns, rattling percussion—that coalesced into teenage symphonies, never overwhelming the material or passionate vocals."[12]

With those kinds of credentials, it seemed like Spector might be able to deliver that sought-after hit single. But his working style clashed with the Ramones'.

"Phil insisted that we play songs over and over. The entire process took only three weeks, but in Ramones time it was interminable," Joey said.[13]

Marky noted that the difference in working styles caused some irritation. "John and Dee Dee were used to working fast, and Phil worked at his own pace, which really frustrated John and Dee Dee because of how things were working."[14]

Johnny didn't like working with Spector, calling the process "painfully slow and stressful."[15]

"He wasn't a pleasant person," Johnny said of Spector. "There were demons inside of him. I had a hard time. My father died in the middle of the album, and that along with Phil's basic unpleasantness . . . it was hard. He was trying to separate Joey from the rest of the band constantly. Joey, Joey, Joey. He was trying to divide the band, and we didn't need that."[16]

Not only was Spector's working style different, but he was a challenging personality. Spector brandished guns at the

Ramones during the sessions. Fed up with it all, Johnny left partway through the production of the album.[17]

"I had left because of the stress I was under," Johnny said. "And once they were going to bring in an orchestra to play on 'Baby I Love You,' I said, 'There's no point in my playing on this song because my specialty was not called for on this one.' Once they started bringing in an orchestra—I ain't playing with no orchestra. That's not me."[18]

The pairing of Spector with the Ramones paid off on some songs, "Do You Remember Rock 'n' Roll Radio" and "Rock 'n' Roll High School." Joey's voice soars on the gentle songs, "Danny Says" and the aforementioned "Baby I Love You," which was a hit for the Ronettes.

The album did have some commercial success—it was the band's highest-charting album—but the pop sound was not well received by many fans.[19]

After *End of the Century,* the Ramones made another change—they changed management. When their contract with comanagers Danny Fields and Linda Stein expired, they signed with new manager Gary Kurfirst. By this time in their career, the Ramones began to get fed up with the music business.

"Things should have changed four years ago—then I thought the whole music business would be 'revolutionized,'" Johnny said. "I looked around and I thought that us and the Sex Pistols were the two best bands at what we were doin'.

And it was, uh, naïve thinking that why shouldn't the two best bands be the two biggest bands."[20]

Johnny continued: "I reali[z]ed soon after that the music business wanted to suppress the whole thing because they didn't understand it. And they didn't want their old things to go out because they didn't know who was good out of this new stuff—they don't know what's good until it sells, then it's 'Heeyyy! You guys are good, you sold a million records!' Otherwise, you're just a problem to them, they don't know how to promote you."[21]

The Ramones returned to the studio in January 1981 to record the *Pleasant Dreams* album. Producer Graham Gouldman, who played with the band 10cc and who had written songs for the Yardbirds and the Hollies, produced *Pleasant Dreams*. Turmoil within the band was growing. Dee Dee's drug addiction was in full swing, and Marky and Joey were developing alcohol problems. Johnny was frustrated with Dee Dee musically and Joey personally.[22]

The band's songwriting had become a source of tension as well. For the first time, the songwriting was credited to individual members. On the earlier albums, all of the songs had been credited to the entire group no matter who wrote them. Johnny wasn't satisfied with the songs on *Pleasant Dreams*. "I knew going in that this was not going to be the type of album

By 1981, there was tension among the band members.

I wanted," he said. "It really could have used another two or three punk songs."[23]

It was during this period that the conflict between Johnny's commitment to hard-driving rock music and Joey's pop sensibilities began to become visible. "All I want to do is keep our fans happy and not sell out," Johnny said. "I'm fighting that within the band. They are trying to go lighter, looking for ways to be more commercial. I'm against the band doing that."[24]

Joey, on the other hand, wanted to embrace his own pop-loving personality. He told Scott Isler from *Trouser Press* in 1982: "By *Road to Ruin* [and] *End of the Century*, I was doing the majority of the songwriting. I started feeling that the Ramones were faceless; there were no individual identities in the band. It worked in the beginning, but as time went on it really started bugging me. Everything I wrote, the band would take credit for. I wanted my individual identity."[25]

In general, the members of the band weren't getting along. "I don't think Joey, Dee Dee or I were talking to each other," said Johnny. "You can go on tour and play your shows with no one talking—it's a job, and you don't have to like everyone you go to work [with]. But when you make a record it really helps if the band is getting along."[26]

Joey said things had changed in the band by the time of *Pleasant Dreams*. "In the early days, we'd be on the road almost 365 days a year. It probably got us really tight, but at the same time it caused a lot of friction and tension," he said. "It was a real rocky time. It probably would have split up most bands."[27]

It was during this period that a falling-out developed between Joey and Johnny that would never heal. Joey had fallen in love with a woman named Linda Danielle. They dated for a while, but eventually she left Joey for Johnny.

Road manager Monte Melnick said, "Joey was devastated. It affected him deeply. Johnny knew it was bad and kept Linda totally hidden from that point on. She didn't come to many shows and if she did he'd hide her in the back; she wouldn't come backstage. He'd run out to meet her and leave as soon as they were done."[28]

Joey harbored a deep grudge against Johnny, who eventually married Linda.

"Johnny crossed the line with me concerning my girlfriend at the time, who he happened to like a little too much, creating total conflict with me in our close-knit situation called the Ramones. He destroyed the relationship and the band right there," Joey said.[29]

Johnny, on the other hand, believed that the falling-out between the two of them had deeper sources. "Joey made more of an issue over it because she left him for me. If she hadn't, he wouldn't have even been talking about her and saying how much he loved her because he wouldn't have been obsessed about it."[30]

In *Rolling Stone,* reviewer David Fricke called *Pleasant Dreams* "the Ramones' state-of-the-union message, an impassioned display of irrepressible optimism and high-amp defiance laced with bitterness over what they see as corporate sabotage of their rock & roll fantasies."[31]

NME reviewer Cynthia Rose also loved the album. "It's great to hear a Ramones LP on which their stand as possibly the last true individuals in America produces real and appropriate dividends; if there's any justice this album will win new friends and influence new people. Certainly it will cement Joey's heroic stature as a vocalist . . . he *follows through* on every note of every track," she wrote.[32]

By the time the Ramones' next album, *Subterranean Jungle,* was released in May 1983, Johnny's punk-rock vision had won out over Joey's pop dreams.

"I knew the band had to be focused and stop worrying about getting played [on the radio] and just make good Ramones records," Johnny said.[33]

Even Joey acknowledged that *Subterranean Jungle* was a return to form for the Ramones.

Joey said:

I guess I felt a little short-changed before. I was just writin' a lotta diverse stuff and maybe I felt I was gonna get restricted, I dunno. Now that we've done it and we've been playing around for about a month, though, we're unanimous. 'Cause it has that real edge again, it has a real powerful sound—somethin' we lost a little on the last two albums. I love those albums y'know, but this one sorta restates a Ramones vision. And it's because the production is really there at last. I think the vocals are the best I've ever done too.[34]

The relationship between band members seemed to be improving somewhat—at least publicly.

"We'd reached the bottom at that point, but we were on an upswing," said Johnny, adding that the band wasn't speaking between *Pleasant Dreams* and *Subterranean Jungle*. "I wasn't talking to Dee Dee at all, and I really needed him for his lyrics."[35]

Johnny and Dee Dee cowrote "Psycho Therapy," which is one of the Ramones' most popular songs.

"I knew we needed a real 'Ramones song' for the album, and I knew John was depressed about how things were going," Dee Dee said. "He needed that song to get excited about the band again."[36]

Reviewer Cynthia Rose called *Subterranean Jungle* the band's "third masterpiece," alongside *The Ramones* and *Rocket to Russia*. "What you will find is: a brand of misfit soul both truly original and truly viable; some classic love songs perfect enough to transport the dead, yet uncloyed for a moment by nostalgia . . . plus one genuinely *appropriate* update of 'psychedelia,'" she wrote.[37]

But the Ramones continued to have personnel problems. This time it was Marky, whose drinking was getting out of control. Road manager Melnick said, "Marky was the life of the party for a long time until his drinking got out of hand. After a while he was smashed all the time. . . . The band was getting upset."[38]

By this time, his alcoholism had gotten so bad that he committed the ultimate sin—he missed a concert. "At one point, I even missed a show," Marky said. "We were in Cleveland, and I stayed an extra night with a friend and woke up the next day partied out."[39]

Instead of making his plane to Virginia, Marky spent the day getting drunk with baseball legend Roger Maris. "After that I was supposed to get to the airport and I was already late and they wondered where . . . I was. So I was going to rent a private plane, and they wouldn't take me because I was too drunk, and I missed the show. The crowd went crazy and wrecked the place, so we had to make it up a month or two later. That's one of the things alcohol was doing to me," Marky said.[40]

Marky was fired in early 1983, with Richie Ramone taking over. The new drummer pumped up the already relentless pace of the Ramones' music.

"I've always drummed in their style—steady and hard-hitting—but it was difficult working myself up to the speed. There are three speeds in the Ramones: fast, pretty fast, and very fast."[41]

The next album, *Too Tough to Die,* was released in October 1984—the band's tenth anniversary. It marked even more of a return to basics for the band.

Johnny said: "As we got ready to make Too Tough To Die, we were focused in the same direction, and it made a difference. We knew we needed to get back to the kind of harder material we'd become known for. The pop stuff hadn't really worked, and we knew we were much better off doing what we did best."[42]

Dee Dee agreed with Johnny's assessment. "I was glad we'd tried to do different things," Dee Dee said. "But we all knew we really needed to make a really mental Ramones album; something that spoke from inside our brain and sounded natural."[43]

One of the reasons the album seemed like a return to form is that it was coproduced by Tommy Ramone and Ed Stasium, who hadn't worked with the band since 1978's *Road to Ruin.*

"I want to just produce and help write songs," said Tommy, "and I did that for a while, but then not being around the guys all the time, and getting involved in other projects, we just kind of drifted apart. But I always went to see them when they were playing in New York, and Dee Dee just called me up one day and asked if I wanted to work with them

In 1983, Richie Ramone took over on drums.

again, and I said 'Sure.' It was that simple. At least it started that simple."[44]

Dee Dee said it felt good to work with Tommy again. "Tommy always knew what we should sound like, and I think we always sounded the best on the albums he worked on," Dee Dee said. "The whole 'less is more' thing, Tommy was a big part of that. . . . [H]e was always able to kind of translate what we did when it came time to get it down on tape."[45]

Dee Dee wrote a lot. "I remember Joey wasn't feeling well while we were getting ready to make the album," Dee Dee said. "Johnny and I were at the studio a lot together, and things kind of clicked between us for the first time in a long time."[46]

Dee Dee's songs began to touch on political themes for the first time. While President Ronald Reagan was in office, cold-war tensions between the United States and the Soviet Union had increased. The Soviet Union, composed of a group of republics, was led by Russia and governed by a single Communist government. "I was forming some opinions about needing some peace in the world," Dee Dee said. "I could feel a lot of violence and hostility in the air, and I needed to try and say something about it."[47]

Joey also was upbeat about the album. "This is the first time in awhile that everyone's been really happy and healthy," he said. "I mean, we been workin' regularly for awhile now, we finished the record in August and things have been great since."[48]

In 1985, the band recorded a single, "Bonzo Goes to Bitburg." President Reagan—who once made a movie with a monkey costar called *Bedtime for Bonzo*—visited a military cemetery in Bitburg, Germany, where Nazi soldiers were buried. Joey—who was Jewish—was outraged. "Everyone told him not to go," he said, "and he went anyway. It embarrassed America and it was a real slap in the face."[49]

The next album, *Animal Boy,* was released in July 1986 and received mixed reviews. *New York Times* critic Jon Pareles named *Animal Boy* the "Rock Album of the Week," writing that "they speak up for outcasts and disturbed individuals . . . and worry about drug users and politics." Pareles noted that the band was straying from its formula. "*Animal Boy* isn't pure, speedy punk," he wrote, "it also includes heavy-metal tunes and even a blatant candidate for rock-radio airplay—the ballad 'She Belongs to Me.'" Even so, Pareles seemed to think the band was staying true to itself. "Whether or not they sneak into the top 40, the Ramones aren't geared to sell out," he wrote.[50]

Rolling Stone critic David Fricke called *Animal Boy* "non-stop primal fuzz pop that rivals *Ramones Leave Home* and *Rocket to Russia* for gonzo chuckles."[51]

Fricke added that "[t]he Ramones . . . are still alive and thrashing. They have stayed true to their original CBGB clatter and goofy sense of adolescent humor and at the same time developed the wit and the will to take on larger issues. . . . Rock & roll has a lot to thank the Ramones for, but *Animal Boy* proves they still have a lot more to give."[52]

The next album, 1987's *Halfway to Sanity* is, by most accounts, the Ramones' worst album. "*Halfway to Sanity* had even less to offer than the mediocre *Animal Boy*. Hampered by the Ramones' lack of direction and limited financial resources, [producer Daniel] Rey struggled to impart his natural enthusiasm for the band. But songs like 'I Wanna Live' and 'Go Li'l Camaro Go' and 'Bop 'Til You Drop' are Ramones-by-numbers, imprinted with the hallmark of a band contractually obligated to make Just Another Album," wrote author Dick Porter.[53]

Veteran rock critic Robert Christgau lamented that "a great band has finally worn down into a day job for night people."[54]

Richie felt underappreciated in the band and began to ask for more money. "With the Ramones, I was Richie Ramone when you wanted me to be, but then I was just a hired guy when you wanted me to be," he said. Richie's main complaint was that he didn't get a share of the money the band made from selling T-shirts at concerts, even though his name was on the shirts. "I felt I was due, I wasn't asking for the world, I felt I should get a little bit of that t-shirt money."[55]

Richie threatened to leave the band if they didn't give him more money, but they fired him instead. He was replaced

at first by Blondie drummer Clem Burke (who adopted the name Elvis Ramone). Although a talented drummer, Burke couldn't adapt to the Ramones style and only lasted two shows with the band.

"He did his best but he didn't have the right style. He was too soft and didn't play what we needed," Johnny said.[56]

The Ramones turned to former drummer Marky, who had quit drinking by this time.

"When I came back I was sober," Marky said. "I didn't want to be treated different, I didn't want them walking on eggshells. I just did what I had to do. They tried Clem Burke and he couldn't cut it. So they called me—I went into the studio and that was it. Nothing changed except me. Being straight is so much better: for 80 minutes you have to play 16th notes constantly on the hi-hat [cymbal used for keeping time], and be ready for those '1-2-3-4s.' You need to be aware of what's going on around you."[57]

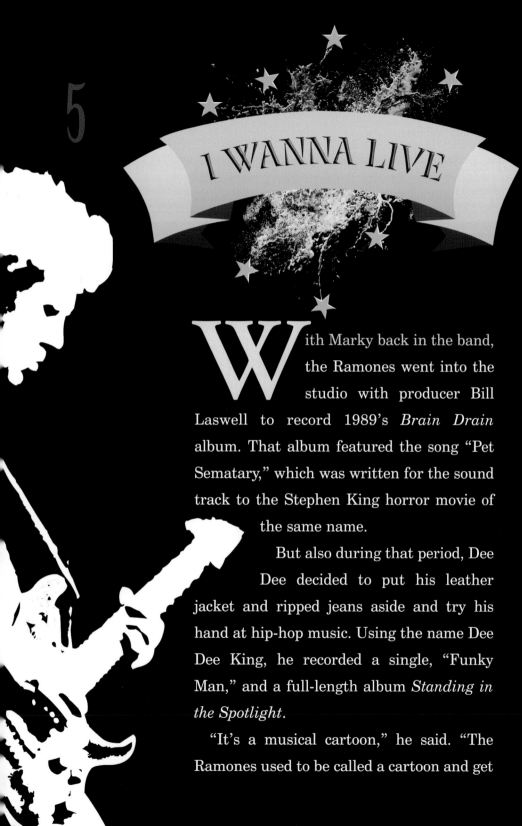

5 I WANNA LIVE

With Marky back in the band, the Ramones went into the studio with producer Bill Laswell to record 1989's *Brain Drain* album. That album featured the song "Pet Sematary," which was written for the sound track to the Stephen King horror movie of the same name.

But also during that period, Dee Dee decided to put his leather jacket and ripped jeans aside and try his hand at hip-hop music. Using the name Dee Dee King, he recorded a single, "Funky Man," and a full-length album *Standing in the Spotlight*.

"It's a musical cartoon," he said. "The Ramones used to be called a cartoon and get

Marky Ramone was back in the band in 1989.

really offended, but I always kind of liked the cartoon image. I'm a big comic-book fan, and I kind of look at life-art-music as comic pop art."[1]

Dee Dee continued to struggle with his addictions to alcohol and heroin. "I'd clean up off one drug and end up on another," he said. "I have an addictive personality. I was kicking dope and praying and praying, getting down on my knees. I got so angry. Why me? Why do I have to be cursed like this? In the long run, I figure it had to happen slow." Even though he found sobriety a struggle, Dee Dee said: "I really believe in it. Sobriety is a gift of God."[2]

He acknowledged that the other Ramones didn't like his hip-hop dreams, but he said he was committed to the band. "Even if 'Standing in the Spotlight' went platinum I wouldn't leave the band. It's fun for me; it's my identity."[3]

A few months later, Dee Dee changed his mind. He quit the Ramones.

"It was pretty unexpected," Joey said. "We didn't have the slightest idea what he was doing. He was sort of scheming for a while. One thing about Dee Dee was that he was very self-centered and I think the whole thing just went to his head—people telling him he's wonderful."[4]

The Ramones held auditions for a new bass player. One bassist in particular caught Johnny's attention—Christopher Ward, who became C. J. Ramone. When he auditioned for the

Ramones, C. J. was AWOL (absent without leave) from the Marine Corps.

"I enlisted because I was having a lot of problems, doing a lot of drugs," C. J. said. "I was doing them just to do them, and I knew I needed a real strict change in my life."[5]

But his status with the Marines jeopardized his ability to play with the Ramones.

"I was actually waiting on a discharge, so it wasn't like I deserted," C. J. said. "They [the Marines] kept trying to send me out to Japan and I knew once I got there, it would be awfully hard to get a discharge."[6]

He rehearsed with the Ramones a couple of times while they auditioned some seventy-five bass players. "Once I started to feel like I was going to get the job, I called them up to find out what I had to do. They arrested me and threw me in the [brig]," C. J. said. "So, the first night I'm in jail I get a phone call from Johnny saying for me to do my time, and when I get out I've got a job. I got out five weeks later and went on tour with the band. . . . In the real early photographs you see of me . . . I've got a bandana around my head cause they just shaved it from the [brig]. I was literally just a week out of jail."[7]

Joey was cheerful about the addition of C. J. to the band. "With Dee Dee, there was a lotta hostility and friction near the end," Joey said. "What happened was he got back into drugs, and was a real mess. We hope he pulls his life together, but

Fred Gwynne played "Jud Crandall" in Stephen King's
Pet Sematary. The album sound track featured a song by

he's gotta do it himself. Now with C. J., it's fun again, it's never been better than it is now. I mean, he's a young kid and a huge Ramones fan and he still can't believe he's in the band! He's adding his own energy and style, and we're harder, tougher and faster, and there's new vitality and spirit in the whole thing."[8]

The band recorded *Mondo Bizarro,* which was released in 1992. It was the group's first record for manager Gary Kurfirst's new label, Radioactive Records. *Rolling Stone* reviewer Dave Thompson wrote that "[t]he Ramones sound fiercer than they have in years on *Mondo Bizarro.*"[9]

Dee Dee relocated to Detroit and started a band called the Chinese Dragons. He continued to write songs for the Ramones, but didn't seem to regret his decision to leave the band. "I ran for my life, for my self, from my life," he said "It was like leaving the Mafia. That was a rough band to get out of. It'll always be following me around. . . . I have no friends, I have no family, the only hope I can have is to forget it. . . . But the Ramones really didn't leave me stranded. I'm not miserable. Something happened."[10]

He continued to struggle to maintain his sobriety. "Drugs make everything worse," Dee Dee said. "And it's humiliating. I was under the rule of them and they were the boss. They're not an alternative to depression; they make it worse. We all find that out. . . . Most of all, I feel like I've been given a break by God or something."[11]

In 1994, the Ramones celebrated their twentieth anniversary as a band. The band was still chugging along—even making an animated appearance on *The Simpsons*—but signs of weariness were starting to show. Johnny in particular began to make noises about breaking up the group.

"I'm just taking it one year at a time. I know I want to do it for '94, it's our 20th year. But the longest I can see doing it is two more years," Johnny said.[12]

Joey also saw that the end was near. "I don't want to be negative, but I've kind of had my fill," he said.[13]

Even though he was feeling worn out, Joey said he thought the band could go on if they wanted it to. "I complain about it, but I really do enjoy it. For me, the Ramones are like the best therapy. But it's nice to have a life," he said.[14]

The Ramones released a new studio album *Adios Amigos* in April 1995. The title—Spanish for "goodbye, friends"—was another indication that the band was saying farewell.

"I'm stopping," Johnny said. "I don't want to become the Rolling Stones or the Who. Why don't these people stop? Can't they live without the attention and the applause? We're still able to play at the level fans expect. I want to quit while we're still good."[15]

Johnny was looking forward to retirement, telling journalists that he planned to move to California and enjoy life.

He had no desire to do new musical projects, saying that "if I'm going to be in music, I'm might as well stay in the Ramones. It's just time to try to move onto something else."[16]

Unlike Johnny, Joey seemed to have conflicting feelings about the band's end. He was aware of the Ramones' impact on the rock world.

"I think we're leaving [a] historical legacy," Joey said. "We really changed rock 'n' roll. When we came out in '74, rock 'n' roll was pretty much dead. . . . It was totally synthetic. All the fun was totally gone. We rocked the boat, you know what I mean?"[17]

"It's simple, but effective," Joey continued. "The greatest art or music was always simple, but effective. I mean Andy Warhol's soup cans were simple, but effective. The best rock 'n' roll appears simple, whether it be Buddy Holly or Little Richard or the Beatles or the Stones or the Who or the Stooges."[18]

The Ramones planned a final concert in Buenos Aires, Argentina, which Joey said was the band's strongest territory. "It's like total insanity. It's like we're a cross between the Beatles and the pope," he said.[19]

Instead of ending with that March gig, the band decided to accept a slot on the alternative rock Lollapalooza summer tour, playing with bands like Metallica and Soundgarden.

The band played its final concert on August 6, 1996, at the Palace in Los Angeles. Dee Dee joined the Ramones

The Ramones in 1996 (back row: Johnny Ramone and C. J. Ramone; front row: Marky Ramone and Joey Ramone).

onstage for the first time since he quit the band in 1989. Members of the bands Pearl Jam, Rancid, Soundgarden, and Motorhead sat in with the Ramones during the seventy-minute set.[20]

Despite the special guests, the final show seemed like a letdown to some. It seemed strange for the Ramones to play their final show in Los Angeles rather than New York City. "The way it ended, with everyone walking away at the end of the night, was kind of fitting. I didn't even say goodbye to anyone," C. J. said.[21]

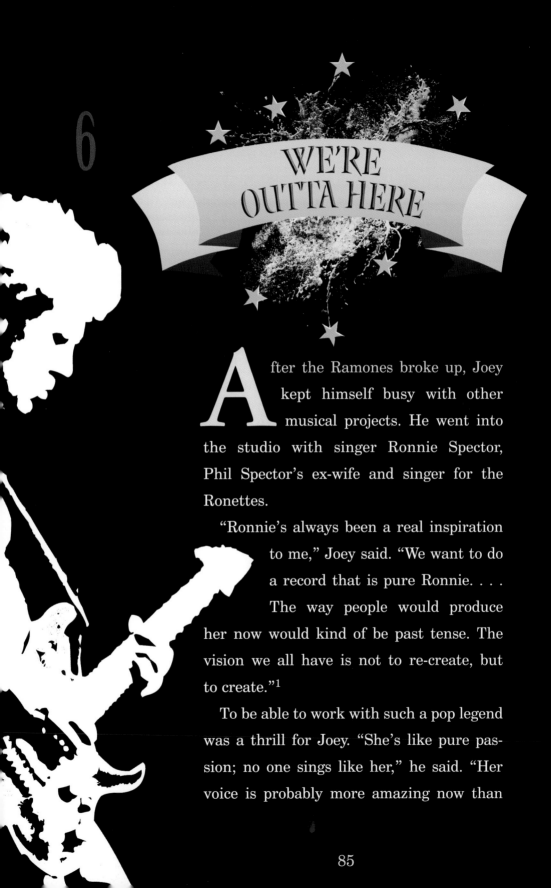

6 WE'RE OUTTA HERE

After the Ramones broke up, Joey kept himself busy with other musical projects. He went into the studio with singer Ronnie Spector, Phil Spector's ex-wife and singer for the Ronettes.

"Ronnie's always been a real inspiration to me," Joey said. "We want to do a record that is pure Ronnie. . . . The way people would produce her now would kind of be past tense. The vision we all have is not to re-create, but to create."[1]

To be able to work with such a pop legend was a thrill for Joey. "She's like pure passion; no one sings like her," he said. "Her voice is probably more amazing now than it's ever been. She just is totally genuine and has that street credibility. She's the original bad girl; before there was Courtney Love or anybody there was Ronnie Spector and she retains that. It's really enjoyable working with her."[2]

The Ramones may have broken up in 1996, but the band's legacy continued to grow. Within a few years after the break-up, the Ramones would receive one of the recording industry's greatest honors, and Joey, Dee Dee, and Johnny would all pass away.

In 1995, Joey was diagnosed with a type of cancer called lymphoma. The illness was kept secret from the public.[3] "To have behaved any other way would have been un-Ramone-like," wrote biographer Everett True.[4]

"We found out he was sick just before Lollapalooza," Johnny said. "We were told that lymphoma is very treatable through medication, but then the complications set in."[5]

Joey tried to keep busy despite his illness, according to his friend and chiropractor Dr. James Forester.

"Joey coped with the reality of cancer like the champion that he was. He always did as much as he possibly could in a day. When it came to his music, he loved immersing himself in it. He was tireless," Forester said.[6]

Joey began recording a solo album with Andy Shernoff from the punk band the Dictators and occasional Ramones producer Daniel Rey. In 2000, Joey performed a Ramones medley during a Christmas show he hosted at a club called the Continental in New York. Shortly after that, he slipped on some ice, fell, and broke his hip. The treatment he received for his broken hip wore him down, and he succumbed to his cancer.[7]

Joey died April 15, 2001. "He was a perfect instrument of those songs and those words and that speed and that energy," said first manager Danny Fields. "He never screamed, never waved his arms around. He stood in one place and delivered. It was so tasteful."[8]

Ronnie Spector issued a statement: "I am devastated to lose a friend and collaborator," she wrote. "Rock 'n' roll lost its most generous soul in Joey."[9]

Joey's funeral was attended by Tommy and C. J. Ramone, as well as Debbie Harry and Joan Jett. But neither Johnny nor Dee Dee showed up.

Dee Dee was on tour in the Netherlands when Joey died. His wife, Barbara, told him the news over the phone. "I kept my emotions to myself after that. I stayed in my room so no one could see how sad I was," Dee Dee wrote.[10]

Johnny was at home in California, but his rift with Joey had never healed, so he stayed home. "I wasn't going to travel all the way to New York, but I wouldn't have gone anyway," Johnny said. "I wouldn't want him coming to my funeral, and I wouldn't want to hear from him if I were dying. I'd only want to see my friends. Let me die and leave me alone. . . . We had a job together. Doesn't mean I have to like him."[11]

Joey would have turned fifty on May 19, 2001—just a month after he died. A memorial birthday party was held for him in a sold-out Hammerstein Ballroom in New York. The party featured performances by Blondie, Cheap Trick, and the Damned. There were also video tributes from Joan Jett, Replacements singer Paul Westerberg, members of the Talking Heads, and Metallica drummer Lars Ulrich.

Journalist Michael Azerrad wrote that "the Ramones embodied punk's inclusiveness, one of it's most attractive—and radical—aspects. Anybody could play great rock music. . . . So it was perfect when a huge Ramones banner was unfurled, an instrumental version of 'I Wanna Be Sedated' came booming over the sound system, and just about everybody sang along. Yes, anybody could do it."[12]

Joey's solo album, *Don't Worry About Me,* was released in February 2002. It featured a touching cover of Louis Armstong's "What a Wonderful World"—a song that showed off the singer's optimism.

"He actually had a very positive attitude," Rey said. "When you're Joey Ramone, you have to. His whole life was an uphill battle. He was like 6 foot tall in seventh grade. And you can imagine when he said he wanted to be a rock star, a few people must have questioned it."[13]

The street in front of CBGB's—corner of the Bowery and

The corner of Bowery and Second Street in New York City was named Joey Ramone Place in 2003.

Second Street in New York City's East Village—was named Joey Ramone Place in 2003. The street was renamed in Joey's honor after a sixteen-year-old girl started a letter-writing campaign and enlisted the help of Hilly Kristal and Arturo Vega.[14]

"This is so satisfying," Vega said. "Joey deserves it. The Ramones deserve it. It's not that common that underdogs like the Ramones get this type of recognition and honor."[15]

The Ramones were inducted into the Rock and Roll Hall of Fame in March 2002. None of the Ramones performed during the show. Dee Dee wrote: "Marky told me that he'd talked to John and John said that he refused to play the Hall of Fame as a tribute to Joey Ramone. He said that he loved the Ramones too much to insult their memory by playing in a watered down version of the band without the original lead singer."[16] Green Day played Ramones songs instead. Pearl Jam singer Eddie Vedder inducted the band, saying the band was "armed with two-minute songs that they rattled off like machine-gun fire. It was enough to change the earth's revolution, or at least the music of the time. It was an assault."[17]

Dee Dee stole the show with his induction speech by saying simply: "Hi, I'm Dee Dee Ramone, and I'd like to congratulate myself, and thank myself, and give myself a big pat

Dee Dee Ramone, Johnny Ramone, Tommy Ramone, and Marky Ramone hold their awards after the Ramones were inducted into the Rock and Roll Hall of Fame in 2002.

on the back. Thank you, Dee Dee, you're very wonderful. I love you."

He looked healthy in the TV broadcast, so it was a surprise when he died of a heroin overdose three months later.

Johnny reflected on Dee Dee, describing him as "a very unique character, the most influential punk rock bassist. He set the standard that all punk rock bassists look to."[18]

Johnny said Dee Dee's songs were his favorites, commenting that they "weren't like anything else, just crazy, crazy stuff. . . . I don't know of anything else like it. He was a great lyricist. I'd write something like say, 'Wart Hog,' and I'd give it to Dee Dee and go here's a song called 'Wart Hog.' And he'd have the lyrics down and he'd just open up his book and just start singing a page out of his book of lyrics. He was really prolific as far as coming up with the lyrics constantly, and I think he influenced every bassist who came to see him play."[19]

Johnny said he last saw Dee Dee two weeks before the bassist died. The former bandmates met for lunch and ran into each other at a Los Angeles record store. "We would see each other here and there. As far as I knew everything was fine, and I didn't know anything was wrong," Johnny said. "Of course, there were different periods of time where you could have expected something like this to happen, but Dee Dee was always a survivor and so it came as a shock."[20]

In the *New York Times* obituary, Jon Perales took notice

of Dee Dee's songwriting, noting that he "had a gift for writing the kind of terse, tuneful songs that made the Ramones a worldwide influence on rock. He wrote punk-rock standards including 'Teenage Lobotomy' and 'Rockaway Beach,' songs that distilled frustration, humor and pleasure into a few words and a few chords. His later songs, like 'Poison Heart' and 'Too Tough to Die,' grew darker but no less concise."[21]

Dee Dee struggled with drug addiction his whole adult life. He frequently would kick drugs and then relapse.

"If you use heroin," wrote Dee Dee, "you catch a habit and end up a slave to the drug. Sooner or later you start to lead a double life and lie for drugs and dollars until you eventually become consumed by the whole experience."[22]

That darkness helped make Dee Dee's art compelling, but it also meant there were frequent times when he was depressed.

"He was really the ultimate punk," said Arturo Vega. "He always did what he wanted, and he never settled for anything. He should be remembered as somebody that showed us how much fun it was and how much it hurt to be a real punk."[23]

Legs McNeil, echoed Vega's sentiments, saying, "I think it takes really disturbed people to make great rock and roll, and Dee Dee was a greatly disturbed person. I don't think he had a peaceful day on the planet."[24]

Johnny began battling prostate cancer in 1999. Much like Joey's cancer, the illness had been kept secret from the public.

But Marky spilled the beans about the seriousness of Johnny's illness to *Rolling Stone*. "Johnny's been a champ in confronting this, but at this point I think the chances are slim," he said.[25]

Marky told the magazine he was speaking out because of an outpouring of concern from people wondering what was happening with his former bandmate. "I've been getting so much email from people and from papers and magazines wanting to know what was up I had to take it upon myself to say something, because eventually John won't be in any condition to say or do anything," Marky said.[26]

Johnny spoke with *Rolling Stone* journalist Charles M. Young about his cancer. "It only hurts when I sit down or stand up," Johnny said. "You just have to make the best of it. Sometimes you wonder, 'Is this worth it?' I don't know. They tell me I'm doing better. It's just a matter of getting over all these side effects. There's always something, though. I'm always sick."[27]

In the interview he was reflective. "It's hard to say if I was having any fun, ever," Johnny said. "I just wanted to do nothing. Have dinner, relax, not be in pain—these things are enjoyable now. I've had a good life. I'd like to live. I'd like to feel better. But I've had a great run. I've done a lot of stuff and left a mark."[28]

He knew the end of his life was near. "This is going to get

me," he told a reporter from the *New York Daily News*. "I just don't know when."[29]

Johnny died in September 2004. When he died, he was surrounded by his wife, Linda, Pearl Jam singer Eddie Vedder, and Rob Zombie. Johnny was remembered as the force that kept the Ramones together for so many years.

"They carved out that 22-year career mostly on Johnny's willpower," said C. J.

PATTI SMITH PLAYED AT CBGB'S ON CLOSING NIGHT.

"He made sure they kept touring, he decided the pace of the set and what songs would be played. He made it happen."[30]

Marky also noted Johnny's musical skills, which were greater than he often received credit for.

"John kept things in control when they could have spun out of control very easily," said Marky. "I always admired his guitar playing. He was the originator of the down-stroke eighth-note guitar style, which is very difficult to do for hours on end like he did playing in the Ramones."[31]

Sex Pistols bassist Glen Matlock also lauded Johnny's guitar style. "Johnny had the guitar sound that launched a thousand bands," he said. "Many bands tried to emulate it, but they never got it right."[32]

In his autobiography, Dee Dee wrote that "a Ramones story can't really have a happy ending."[33] And, in some ways, that's true. Not only have the three most visible Ramones died, but CBGB's closed in 2006 and owner Hilly Kristal died of lung cancer in 2007. Original comanager Linda Stein was murdered in 2007. Many of the Ramones' contemporaries have also lost band members.

But even so, the Ramones' heritage lives on. Tommy plays in a country/bluegrass duo called Uncle Monk. C. J. plays with a band called Bad Chopper. Marky remains active, playing with bands Marky Ramone and the Intruders, the Misfits, and Osaka Pop Star. He also has a satellite radio show on Sirius. Marky said he asks himself a few questions when he considers what projects to take on. "Well, the first thing is, is it gonna be fun? The second is, what does it relate to? If it's the Ramones, that's good, because I want to keep the legacy alive," Marky said. "Third is my input into the situation. Like my radio show on Sirius. I pick every song I play. If I couldn't, I wouldn't do it.[34]

The Ramones also live on through merchandise—not just

The Ramones legacy is about getting out there and doing something yourself. This guitar rests on the hand imprints of the band members at the Hollywood Rockwalk in Los Angeles, California,

T-shirts, but flip-flops, shower curtains, pillows, bar stools, board shorts, skateboards, flags, and Converse sneakers "It's sad but true; their deaths brought more interest to the Ramones and made the band bigger," said Johnny's widow, Linda. "I love when I see anyone in Ramones T-shirts," she added. "Johnny did want [them] to be the biggest band in the world."[35]

CBGB's has also lived on in a new form—fashion designer John Varvatos turned it into a boutique, preserving one of the club's original walls intact under glass.

"The whole purpose of coming here was to retain part of the history," Varvatos said, "so that anybody can walk in off the street and experience part of what was here."[36]

But the Ramones' legacy—and the legacy of punk rock—isn't about preserving historical sites. It's about getting out there and doing something yourself. Patti Smith may have said it best the night she played the last set on CBGB's closing night. "There's new kids with new ideas all over the world," she said. "They'll make their own places—it doesn't matter whether it's here or wherever it is."[37]

TIMELINE

1973—CBGB's opens.

1974—Tommy, Joey, Dee Dee, and Johnny form the Ramones; in August, they play their first show at CBGB's.

1975—Ramones are signed to Sire Records.

1976—Ramones release their first album; they play their first concerts in England.

1978—Tommy quits the band, Marky is hired; Ramones film *Rock 'n' Roll High School*.

1980—Ramones record album *End of the Century* with legendary producer Phil Spector.

1983—Marky is fired from the band; he is replaced by Richie.

1987—Richie leaves the Ramones; Marky rejoins.

1989—Dee Dee quits the Ramones to pursue rap career; he is replaced by C. J.

1993—Ramones appear on *The Simpsons*.

1996—Ramones join the Lollapalooza tour; play their last concert in August.

2001—Joey Ramone dies of lymphoma.

2002—Ramones are inducted into Rock and Roll Hall of Fame; Dee Dee Ramone dies of a heroin overdose.

2003—Street in front of CBGB's renamed "Joey Ramone Place."

2004—Johnny Ramone dies of prostate cancer.

DISCOGRAPHY

Albums

1976 *Ramones*

1977 *Leave Home*

Rocket to Russia

1978 *Road to Ruin*

1979 *It's Alive*

1980 *End of the Century*

1981 *Pleasant Dreams*

1983 *Subterranean Jungle*

1984 *Too Tough to Die*

1986 *Animal Boy*

1987 *Halfway to Sanity*

1988 *Ramones Mania*

1989 *Brain Drain*

1992 *Loco Live*

Mondo Bizarro

1993 *Acid Eaters*

1995 *Adios Amigos*

1996 *Greatest Hits Live*

1997 *We're Outta Here!*

1999 *Hey Ho Let's Go! Ramones Anthology*

2005 *Weird Tales of the Ramones*

DVDs

2004 *Ramones Raw*

2005 *End of the Century: The Story of the Ramones*

Rock 'n' Roll High School

2007 *Ramones: It's Alive 1974–1996*

CONCERT TOURS

The Ramones toured relentlessly through their twenty-two-year history. Listed below are how many concerts they played each year they were together.

1974: 30

1975: 46

1976: 80

1977: 147

1978: 139

1979: 158

1980: 155

1981: 96

1982: 69

1983: 97

1984: 86

1985: 89

1986: 83

1987: 104

1988: 111

1989: 96

1990: 125

1991: 98

1992: 94

1993: 113

1994: 95

1995: 111

1996: 69

GLOSSARY

alienation—The feeling of being isolated from others.

antisocial—A person who is inconsiderate, disruptive, or rebellious.

Bowery—A street in Manhattan that was once known as a seedy area filled with bums.

cold war—A conflict between the United States and the Soviet Union that lasted from the end of World War II until the early 1990s. The conflict between those two countries (and their allies) featured tension and military buildup, but no actual fighting.

Communism—A political philosophy in which all property and wealth is owned by the state. In many Communist countries, a single political party has total control of society and government.

delinquent—An antisocial young person.

gourmandizers—A made-up word in the full name of the club CBGB's; a play on the word *gourmand,* which is a person who loves good food and drink to a great degree.

lobotomy—A type of surgery where part of a person's brain is removed.

punk—A loud and aggressive style of music; an insulting word that can mean a lazy, worthless, or arrogant person.

virtuoso—An exceptionally talented musician; a musician with great technique.

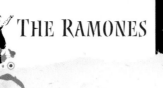

CHAPTER NOTES

Chapter 1: . . .Tomorrow the World

1. *End of the Century: The Story of the Ramones,* DVD, directed by Jim Fields and Michael Gramaglia (2003; Los Angeles: Rhino/Wea, 2005).

2. Ibid.

3. Dick Porter, *Ramones: The Complete Twisted History* (London: Plexus Books, 2004), p. 138.

4. Legs McNeil and Gillian McCain, *Please Kill Me* (New York: Penguin, 1996), p. 320.

5. Max Bell, "Flamin' Groovies/The Ramones/The Stranglers: Roundhouse, London," *NME,* July 10, 1976, <http://www.rocksbackpages.com/article.html?ArticleID=5850> (April 4, 2007).

6. Ibid.

7. Ibid.

8. Max Bell, "The Ramones: 'Waitin' for World War III' Blues," *NME,* July 17, 1976, <http://www.rocksbackpages.com/article.html?ArticleID=5852> (April 4, 2007).

9. Ibid.

10. Mat Snow, "The Flamin' Groovies and The Ramones: London Roundhouse," *NME,* Summer 1976, <http://www.rocksbackpages.com/article.html?ArticleID=4080> (April 4, 2007).

11. Mat Snow, "Meet the Family: Ramones, Blondie,

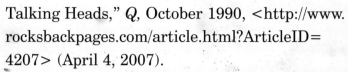

Talking Heads," *Q,* October 1990, <http://www.
rocksbackpages.com/article.html?ArticleID=
4207> (April 4, 2007).

12. Jim Bessman, *Ramones: An American Band* (New
York: St. Martin's Press, 1993), p. 62.

13. McNeil and McCain, p. 231.

14. Ben Sisario, "Johnny Ramone, Pioneer Punk
Guitarist, Is Dead at 55," *New York Times,*
September 17, 2004, p. 25.

15. Heather Burke, "A Pioneer of Punk Rock:
Co-founder of the Ramones," *Bloomberg News,*
September 17, 2004.

16. *Ramones Raw,* DVD, directed by John Cafiero
(Chatsworth, Calif.: Image Entertainment, 2004).

17. Mark Jenkins, "The Ramones: Time to Be
Sedated?" *Washington Post,* August 6, 1995, p. G5.

18. Donna Gaines, The Ramones: *Ramones,* CD liner
notes, Rhino Records.

Chapter 2: Who Are the Ramones?

1. John Leland, "A Star of Anti-Charisma, Joey
Ramone Made Geeks Chic," *New York Times,*
April 22, 2001, <http://query.nytimes.com/gst/
fullpage.html?res=9C03E0DA1330F931A15757C0
A9679C8B63&sec=&spon=&pagewanted=1>
(September 11, 2008).

2. David Fricke, The Ramones: *Loud/Fast* CD liner
notes, Rhino Records.

3. Ibid.

4. Barney Hoskyns and Mat Snow, "The Ramones: Ain't No Stoppin' the Cretins From Boppin!" *NME,* February 16, 1985, <http://www.rocksbackpages. com/article.html?ArticleID=1692> (April 4, 2007).

5. Jim Bessman, *Ramones: An American Band* (New York: St. Martin's Press, 1993), p. 2

6. "Obessive-Compulsive Disorder (OCD)," *National Institute of Mental Health,* April 2, 2008, <http:// www.nimh.nih.gov/health/topics/obsessive-compulsive-disorder-ocd/index.shtml> (September 11, 2008).

7. Monte A. Melnick and Frank Meyer, *On the Road With the Ramones* (London: Omnibus Press, 2007), p. 154.

8. *End of the Century: The Story of the Ramones,* DVD, directed by Jim Fields and Michael Gramaglia (2003; Los Angeles: Rhino/Wea, 2005).

9. Melnick, p. 182.

10. Charles M. Young, "Johnny's Last Stand," *Rolling Stone,* September 16, 2004, <http://www.rolling-stone.com/artists/theramones/articles/story/6485108/johnnys_last_stand> (September 11, 2008).

11. "Culture Shock: Flashpoints: Music and Dance: Elvis Presley," *PBS.org,* n.d., <http://www.pbs.

org/wgbh/cultureshock/flashpoints/music/elvis. html> (September 11, 2008).

12. Phil Sutcliffe, "'We're Just Very Mean, Very Angry People. We're the Real Thing.' The Ramones Get to Phil Sutcliffe," *Sounds,* December 31, 1977, <http://www.rocksbackpages.com/article. html?ArticleID=2018> (September 11, 2008).

13. Bessman, p. 5.

14. Ibid.

15. Dee Dee Ramone, *Lobotomy: Surviving the Ramones* (New York: Thunder's Mouth Press, 2000), pp. 7–8.

16. Ibid., p. 10.

17. Ibid., p. 23.

18. Ibid., pp. 22–23.

19. Melnick, p. 46.

20. *Hey Is Dee Dee Home,* DVD, directed by Lech Kowalski (Oaks, Pa.: Mvd Visual, 2003).

21. Everett True, *Hey Ho, Let's Go: The Story of the Ramones* (London: Omnibus Press, 2002), p. 18.

22. Melnick, p. 21.

23. Bessman, p. 6.

24. Ibid., p. 7.

25. Melnick, p. 26.

26. True, p. 114.

27. Ibid.

28. David Brinn, "Marky Ramone Refuses to be Sedated," *Jerusalem Post,* January 4, 2008, p. 3.

29. True, p. 250.

30. Ibid.

31. Ibid.

32. Steven Mikulan, "Richie Ramone Does West Side Story," *LA Weekly,* August 15, 2007, <http://www.laweekly.com/music/music/richie-ramone-does-west-side-story/17017> (September 11, 2008).

33. Ibid.

34. Ibid.

Chapter 3: Hey Ho Let's Go!

1. Dee Dee Ramone, *Lobotomy: Surviving the Ramones* (New York: Thunder's Mouth Press, 2000), p. 30.

2. Jim Bessman, *Ramones: An American Band* (New York: St. Martin's Press, 1993), p. 7.

3. Ramone, pp. 53–54.

4. Ibid., p. 56.

5. Bessman, p. 19.

6. "Rolling Stone Music Awards '73," *Rolling Stone,* January 17, 1974, p. 11.

7. "World News Roundup," *Rolling Stone,* September 13, 1973, pp. 8–10.

8. *Ramones: The True Story,* DVD (Classic Rock Legends, 2006).

9. Ramone, p. 73.

10. Ibid., p. 76.

11. Legs McNeil and Gillian McCain, *Please Kill Me* (New York: Penguin, 1996), p. 180.

12. Monte A. Melnick and Frank Meyer, *On the Road With the Ramones* (London: Omnibus Press, 2007), p. 133.

13. Melnick, p. 32.

14. *1977: The Coolest Year in Hell,* VH1 documentary, directed by Henry Corra, originally aired August 11, 2007 (Mamaroneck, N.Y.: Firehouse Films, 2007).

15. Ibid.

16. Ibid.

17. Ben Sisario, "Hilly Kristal, 75, Catalyst for Punk at CBGB, Dies," *New York Times,* August 30, 2007, <http://www.nytimes.com/2007/08/30/arts/music/30kristal.html> (September 12, 2008).

18. Ibid.

19. *1977: The Coolest Year in Hell.*

20. Robert Palmer, "A New Life for the Bowery," *New York Times,* April 15, 1977, p. 57.

21. Mat Snow, "Meet the Family: Ramones, Blondie, Talking Heads," *Q,* October 1990, <http://www.rocksbackpages.com/article.html?ArticleID=4207> (April 4, 2007).

22. *1977: The Coolest Year in Hell.*

23. Jon Pareles, "Dee Dee Ramone, Pioneer Punk Rocker, Dies at 50," *New York Times,* June 7, 2002, p. 12.

24. Alan Betrock, "Know Your New York Bands: The Ramones," *Soho Weekly News,* 1975, <http://www.rocksbackpages.com/article.html?ArticleID=6510> (February 27, 2009).

25. Ibid.

26. Ibid.

27. Ibid.

28. Ibid.

29. Everett True, *Hey Ho, Let's Go: The Story of the Ramones* (London: Omnibus Press, 2002), p. 36.

30. Melnick, p. 62.

31. Chris Morris, "Joey Ramone, Punk's First Icon, Dies," *Billboard,* April 28, 2001.

32. Donna Gaines, The Ramones: *Ramones,* CD liner notes, Rhino Records.

33. Ibid.

34. Kris Needs, "The Ramones: *Ramones* (Sire Import)," *ZigZag,* July 1976, <http://www.rocksbackpages.com/article.html?ArticleID=10808> February 27, 2009.

35. Advertisement, *Village Voice,* January 3, 1977, p. 46.

36. Donna Gaines, The Ramones: *Leave Home,* CD liner notes, Rhino Records.

37. Ibid.

38. Mick Farren, "Notes on Minimalism (or Learning to Live With The Ramones)," *NME,* May 23,

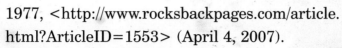

1977, <http://www.rocksbackpages.com/article. html?ArticleID=1553> (April 4, 2007).

39. Gaines, *Leave Home,* CD liner notes.

40. Roy Trakin, "The Ramones: Rockets or Rubberbands?" *New York Rocker,* February 1978, <http://www.rocksbackpages.com/article.html? ArticleID=1810> (April 4, 2007).

41. Gaines, *Leave Home,* CD liner notes.

42. Ibid.

43. Kris Needs, "NY Punk," *ZigZag,* April 1977, <http://www.rocksbackpages.com/article.html? ArticleID=10766> (February 27, 2009).

44. *1977: The Coolest Year in Hell*.

45. Ibid.

46. *End of the Century: The Story of the Ramones,* DVD, directed by Jim Fields and Michael Gramaglia (2003; Los Angeles: Rhino/Wea, 2005).

47. Legs McNeil, The Ramones: *Rocket to Russia,* CD liner notes, Rhino Records.

48. Ibid.

49. Ibid.

50. Ibid.

51. Ibid.

52. *End of the Century,* DVD.

53. Legs McNeil, The Ramones: *Road to Ruin,* CD liner notes, Rhino Records.

54. McNeil, *Rocket to Russia,* CD liner notes.

55. Bessman, p. 90.

Chapter 4: Road to Ruin

1. Monte A. Melnick and Frank Meyer, *On the Road With the Ramones* (London: Omnibus Press, 2007), p. 127.

2. Jim Bessman, *Ramones: An American Band* (New York: St. Martin's Press, 1993), p. 96.

3. Roy Trakin, "Road to Ruin: One Small Step For Man, One Giant Step For The Ramones," *New York Rocker,* September 1978, <http://www.rocksbackpages.com/article.html?ArticleID=3224> (April 4, 2007).

4. Ibid.

5. Charles M. Young, "The Ramones: Road to Ruin," *Rolling Stone,* November 2, 1978, <http://www.rollingstone.com/artists/theramones/albums/album/121860/review/5945084/road_to_ruin> (September 12, 2008).

6. Ibid.

7. Bessman, p. 101.

8. *Rock 'n' Roll High School* Special Edition DVD, directed by Alan Arkush (Burbank, Calif.: Buena Vista Home Entertainment, 2005).

9. Bessman, p. 105

10. *Rock 'n' Roll High School* Special Edition DVD.

11. Ibid.

12. Richie Unterberger and Steve Huey, *All Music Guide*, 4th Edition, ed. Vladimir Bogdanov, Chris

Woodstra, and Stephen Erlewine (San Francisco, Calif.: Backbeat Books, 2001), pp. 380–381.

13. Harvey Kubernick, The Ramones: *End of the Century,* CD liner notes, Rhino Records.

14. Ibid.

15. Colin Devenish, "Johnny Ramone Stays Tough," *Rolling Stone,* June 24, 2002, <http://www.rollingstone.com/artists/theramones/articles/story/5934320/johnny_ramone_stays_tough> (September 12, 2008).

16. Ibid.

17. Everett True, *Hey Ho, Let's Go: The Story of the Ramones* (London: Omnibus Press, 2002), p. 140.

18. Ibid.

19. Kubernick, *End of the Century,* CD liner notes.

20. Cynthia Rose, "The Ramones: The Thinking Men of Pop," *NME,* November 21, 1981, <http://www.rocksbackpages.com/article.html?ArticleID=1213> (April 4, 2007).

21. Ibid.

22. True, p. 162.

23. Ira Robbins, *Pleasant Dreams,* CD liner notes, Rhino Records.

24. Ibid.

25. Ibid.

26. Ibid.

27. True, p. 163.

28. Melnick, p. 173.

29. Andy Gill and Jaan Uhelszki, "The Ramones: *Hey! Ho! Let's Go—The Ramones Anthology,*" *Mojo,* August 1999, <http://www.rocksbackpages. com/article.html?ArticleID=4959> (April 4, 2007).

30. Melnick, p. 177.

31. David Fricke, "The Ramones: *Pleasant Dreams,*" *Rolling Stone,* October 29, 1981, <http://www. rollingstone.com/reviews/album/126169/review/ 6210796/pleasantdreams> (September 12, 2008).

32. Cynthia Rose, "The Ramones: *Pleasant Dreams,*" *NME,* July 11, 1981, <http://www.rocksbackpages. com/article.html?ArticleId=1212> (April 4, 2007).

33. Gil Kaufman, *Subterranean Jungle,* CD liner notes, Rhino Records.

34. Cynthia Rose, "Pal Joey," *NME,* April 16, 1983, <http://www.rocksbackpages.com/article.html? ArticleID=1211> (April 4, 2007).

35. Kaufman, *Subterranean Jungle,* CD liner notes.

36. Ibid.

37. Cynthia Rose, "The Ramones: *Subterranean Jungle* (Sire)," *NME,* 1983, <http://www. rocksbackpages.com/article.html?ArticleID= 1308> (April 4, 2007).

38. Melnick, p. 130.

39. Bessman, p. 126.

40. Ibid.

41. True, p. 192.

42. Billy Altman, The Ramones: *Too Tough To Die,* CD liner notes, Rhino Records.

43. Ibid.

44. Ibid.

45. Ibid.

46. Ibid.

47. Ibid.

48. Cynthia Rose, "The Ramones: Now I Wanna Play My Five-Iron," *NME,* November 10, 1984, <http://www.rocksbackpages.com/article.html? ArticleID=1306> (April 4, 2007).

49. Bessman, p. 131.

50. Jon Pareles, "Pop and Jazz Guide," *New York Times,* June 6, 1986, p. C22.

51. David Fricke, "The Ramones: *Animal Boy,*" *Rolling Stone,* July 17, 1986, <http://www. rollingstone.com/artists/theramones/albums/ album/323069/review/5941801/animal_boy> (September 12, 2008).

52. Ibid.

53. Dick Porter, *Ramones: The Complete Twisted History* (London: Plexus Books, 2004), p. 124.

54. "Ramones," *Robert Christgau,* n.d., <http://www. robertchristgau.com/get_artist.php?name= Ramones> (September 12, 2008).

55. *End of the Century: The Story of the Ramones,* DVD, directed by Jim Fields and Michael Gramaglia (2003; Los Angeles: Rhino/Wea, 2005).

56. Porter, p. 125.

57. True, p. 224.

Chapter 5: I Wanna Live

1. Jim Sullivan, "Dee Dee Ramone's Rap 'n' Roll," *Boston Globe,* April 17, 1989, p. 33.

2. Ibid.

3. Ibid.

4. Jim Sullivan, "Dee Dee Says Bye-Bye," *Boston Globe,* March 2, 1990, <http://www.highbeam.com/doc/1P2-8162861.html> (September 16, 2008).

5. Jim Bessman, *Ramones: An American Band* (New York: St. Martin's Press, 1993), p. 150.

6. Maggie St. Thomas, "One on One: C. J. Ramone," *Concertlivewire.com,* December 3, 2001, <http://www.concertlivewire.com/interviews/ramonecj.htm> (September 12, 2008).

7. Ibid.

8. Chris O'Connor, "Who Would Have Guessed Ramones Would be Musical?" *Toronto Star,* August 5, 1991, p. D5.

9. Dave Thompson, "The Ramones: *Mondo Bizarro,*" *Rolling Stone,* October 29, 1992, <http://www.rollingstone.com/artists/theramones/albums/album/289722/review/5945170/mondo_bizarro> (September 12, 2008).

10. Jim Sullivan, "Dee Dee Ramone Comes Out

Rocking: Music Review Dee Dee Ramone and the Chinese Dragons at: Bunratty's Wednesday Night," *Boston Globe,* September 18, 1992, p. 62.

11. Ibid.

12. Ira Robbins, "The Ramones at 20 Face the Future," *Newsday,* February 5, 1994, p. E3.

13. Ibid.

14. Ibid.

15. Edna Gundersen, "Ramones to Hang up Punk Mantle," *USA Today,* July 11, 1995, p. 8D.

16. Neil Davidson, "One-Two-Three-Four, Ramones Will Soon Be No More," *Ottawa Citizen,* August 1, 1995, p. C8.

17. Jim Sullivan "The Ramones' Last Tour," *Boston Globe*, February 11, 1996, p. 53.

18. Ibid.

19. Ibid.

20. Jim Bessman, "Ramones May Be 'Outta Here,' But Their Finale Lives On Video," *Billboard,* January 17, 1998.

21. Monte A. Melnick and Frank Meyer, *On the Road With the Ramones* (London: Omnibus Press, 2007), p. 257.

Chapter 6: We're Outta Here

1. Melinda Newman, "Neil Young Joins H.O.R.D.E.; Ronnie Asks Joey to 'Be My Baby'," *Billboard,* February 1, 1997.

2. Richard Skanse, "I Don't Wanna Grow Up—Or Be a Ramone Again," *Rolling Stone,* July 23, 1999, <http://www.rollingstone.com/artists/ theramones/articles/story/5927555/i_dont_wanna_ grow_up__or_be_a_ramone_again> (September 12, 2008).

3. Dick Porter, *Ramones: The Complete Twisted History* (London: Plexus Books, 2004), pp. 137–138.

4. Everett True, *Hey Ho, Let's Go: The Story of the Ramones* (London: Omnibus Press, 2002), p. 300.

5. Charles M. Young, "Johnny's Last Stand," *Rolling Stone,* September 16, 2004, <http://www. rollingstone.com/artists/theramones/articles/ story/6485108/johnnys_last_stand> (September 12, 2008).

6. Monte A. Melnick and Frank Meyer, *On the Road With the Ramones* (London: Omnibus Press, 2007), p. 264.

7. Nicky Parade, "Hey Ho, He's Gone: Farewell Joey Ramone—1951–2001," *Rock's Backpages,* April 21, 2001, <http://www.rocksbackpages.com/article. html?ArticleID=2837> (September 12, 2008).

8. Ann Powers, "Joey Ramone, Punk's Influential Yelper, Dies at 49," *New York Times,* April 16, 2001, p. 6

9. Chris Morris, "Joey Ramone, Punk's First Icon, Dies," *Billboard,* April 28, 2001.

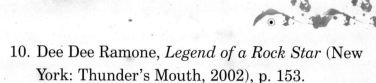

10. Dee Dee Ramone, *Legend of a Rock Star* (New York: Thunder's Mouth, 2002), p. 153.

11. Young.

12. Michael Azerrad, "Joey Ramone's 50th Birthday Bash: Hammerstein Ballroom, New York," *Boston Phoenix,* May 31, 2001, <http://www.rocksbackpages.com/article.html?ArticleID=10059> (April 4, 2007).

13. Jim Farber, "Ramone Alone: Joey's Solo Farewell," *(NY) Daily News,* February 19, 2002.

14. Daniel Wakin, "Hey Ho, Let's Go Downtown to Joey Ramone Place," *New York Times,* November 29, 2003, <http://query.nytimes.com/gst/fullpage.html?res=9B02E6DE123AF93AA15752C1A9659C8B63&scp=1&sq=%22Joey+Ramone+Place%22&st=nyt> (September 12, 2008).

15. Ibid.

16. Dee Dee Ramone, *Lobotomy: Surviving the Ramones* (New York: Thunder's Mouth Press, 2000), p. 183

17. Ramone, *Legend of a Rock Star,* p. 204.

18. Colin Devenish, "Johnny Ramone Stays Tough," *Rolling Stone,* June 24, 2002, <http://www.rollingstone.com/artists/theramones/articles/story/5934320/johnny_ramone_stays_tough> (September 12, 2008).

19. Ibid.

20. Ibid.

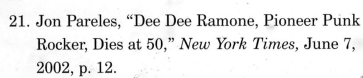

21. Jon Pareles, "Dee Dee Ramone, Pioneer Punk Rocker, Dies at 50," *New York Times,* June 7, 2002, p. 12.

22. Jim Sullivan, "Dee Dee Ramone, 50; Bassist in Trailblazing Punk Rock Band," *Boston Globe,* June 7, 2002, p. C32.

23. Pareles, p. 12.

24. Ibid.

25. Colin Devenish, "Johnny Ramone Has Cancer," *Rolling Stone,* June 15, 2004, <http://www.rollingstone.com/artists/theramones/articles/story/6185029/johnny_ramone_has_cancer> (September 12, 2008).

26. Ibid.

27. Young.

28. Ibid.

29. Jim Farber, "Bye Bye Johnny," *(NY) Daily News,* September 17, 2004, p. 59.

30. Matt Schudel, "Johnny Ramone, Rock-and-Roll Innovator, Dies," *Washington Post,* September 17, 2004, p. B06.

31. Phil Gallo, "Pioneer of Punk Guitar Defined Ramones Sound," *Daily Variety,* September 17, 2004, p. 6.

32. Tamara Conniff and Tom Ferguson, "Guitarist Johnny Ramone Dies of Cancer at 55," *Billboard,* September 25, 2004.

33. Ramone, *Lobotomy,* p. 287.

34. Simona Rabinovitch, "Marky Ramone," *Globe and Mail* (Canada), June 9, 2006, p. R33.

35. David Browne, "Hey! Ho! Let's Shop!" *Spin,* February 2008, p. 36.

36. Ben Sisario, "This Ain't No Nightclub (at Least Not Anymore)," *New York Times,* April 19, 2008, <http://www.nytimes.com/2008/04/19/arts/music/19varv.html> (September 12, 2008).

37. Ben Sisario, "CBGB Brings Down the Curtain With Nostalgia and One Last Night of Rock," *New York Times,* October 16, 2006, <http://www.nytimes.com/2006/10/16/arts/music/16cbgb.html?pagewanted=1> (September 17, 2008).

FURTHER READING

Hayes, Malcolm. *1970s: Turbulent Times*. Milwaukee,
   Wisc.: Gareth Stevens Pub., 2002.

Melnic, Monte, and Frank Meyer. *On the Road With the
   Ramones*. London: Bobcat Books, 2007.

Schaefer, A.R. *Forming a Band*. Mankato, Minn.:
   Capstone High-Interest Books, 2004.

True, Everett. *Hey Ho Let's Go: The Story of the Ramones*.
   London: Omnibus Press, 2005.

INTERNET ADDRESSES

Rock and Roll Hall of Fame and Museum: Ramones
<http://www.rockhall.com/inductee/ramones>

Rolling Stone: The Ramones
<http://www.rollingstone.com/artists/theramones>

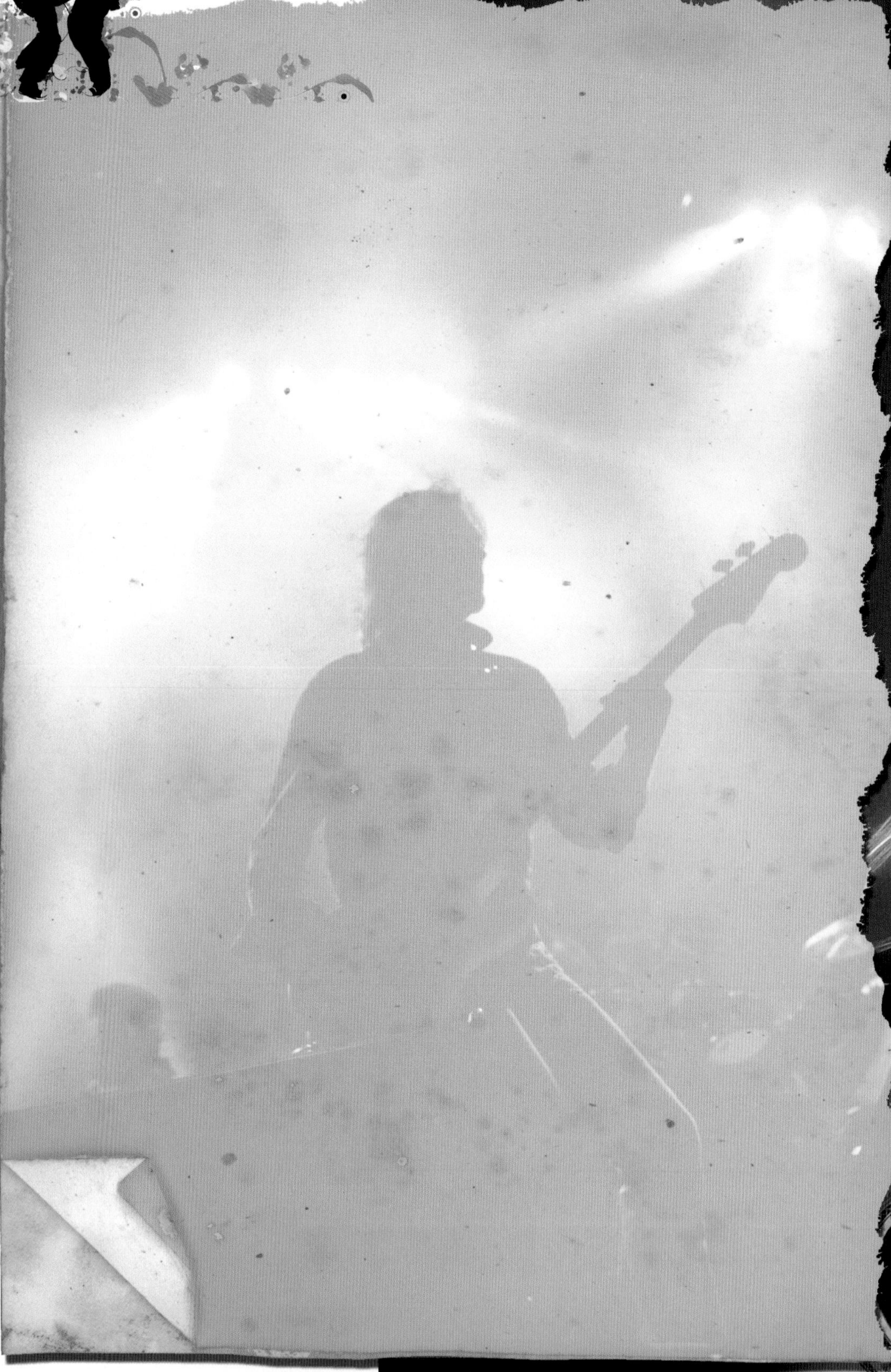

INDEX

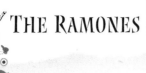